Overbooked and Overwhelmed

Overbooked and Overwhelmed

HOW TO KEEP UP WITH GOD WHEN YOU'RE JUST TRYING TO KEEP UP WITH LIFE

TARA SUN

An Imprint of Thomas Nelson

Overbooked and Overwhelmed

Copyright © 2025 by Tara Sun Snyder

All rights reserved. No portion of this book may be reproduced, stored in a retrieval system, or transmitted in any form or by any means—electronic, mechanical, photocopy, recording, scanning, or other—except for brief quotations in critical reviews or articles, without the prior written permission of the publisher.

Published in Nashville, Tennessee, by Nelson Books, an imprint of Thomas Nelson. Nelson Books and Thomas Nelson are registered trademarks of HarperCollins Christian Publishing, Inc.

Published in association with William K. Jensen Literary Agency, 119 Bampton Court, Eugene, Oregon 97404.

Thomas Nelson titles may be purchased in bulk for educational, business, fundraising, or sales promotional use. For information, please email SpecialMarkets@ThomasNelson.com.

Unless otherwise noted, Scripture quotations are taken from the ESV® Bible (The Holy Bible, English Standard Version®). Copyright © 2001 by Crossway, a publishing ministry of Good News Publishers. Used by permission. All rights reserved. Scripture quotations marked MSG are taken from *The Message*. Copyright © 1993, 2002, 2018 by Eugene H. Peterson. Used by permission of NavPress. All rights reserved. Represented by Tyndale House Publishers, Inc. Scripture quotations marked NIV are taken from the Holy Bible, New International Version®, NIV®. Copyright © 1973, 1978, 1984, 2011 by Biblica, Inc.® Used by permission of Zondervan. All rights reserved worldwide. www.Zondervan.com. The "NIV" and "New International Version" are trademarks registered in the United States Patent and Trademark Office by Biblica, Inc.® Scripture quotations marked NLT are taken from the Holy Bible, New Living Translation. © 1996, 2004, 2015 by Tyndale House Foundation. Used by permission of Tyndale House Publishers, Inc., Carol Stream, Illinois 60188. All rights reserved.

Library of Congress Control Number: 2024060131

Printed in the United States of America

25 26 27 28 29 LBC 5 4 3 2 1

For my parents.

You may never realize just how much you shaped this message—by the way you both live devoted and selflessly served me through the writing process. Thank you for your unending prayers, conversations about this message around the dinner table, and fueling our family with meals and quality time. In countless ways, this book is here because of the two of you.

Contents

One: Discover the Devoted Life 1
Two: The Cost of Distraction.................... 19
Three: Identify Your Cravings 39
Four: Remember Who You Are 59
Five: Choose the Better Portion.................... 79
Six: Prioritize His Presence 99
Seven: The Power of Your Yes and No 119
Eight: A Word for the Weary 137
Nine: More Rhythm, Less Rush 159
Ten: Small Steps of Faithfulness 185

Conclusion.................................... 205
Acknowledgments............................ 211
Notes.. 215
About the Author 219

ONE

Discover the Devoted Life

What you give your attention to is the person you become. Put another way: the mind is the portal to the soul, and what you fill your mind with will shape the trajectory of your character.

JOHN MARK COMER

*H*ot tears streamed down my face as I washed the dishes that were piled high in the sink. It was midnight, and there I was, sobbing over the suds.

My husband, Michael, looked at me in disbelief. "Why are you doing dishes at midnight? You need to go to bed, hon."

"I can't!" I snapped at him as I scrubbed my casserole dish.

"Why?" he asked, caught off guard.

I did my best to quickly wipe away my tears (and snot) and attempted to fake a smile. "If I do go to bed, everything will fall apart."

That was me not all that long ago. I was burned out, stressed out, maxed out, and distracted as all get-out. To some, scrubbing dishes at midnight out of fear of the world falling apart sounds ridiculous, but to others it's painfully relatable. Most of us understand the overwhelm from carrying a staggering number of responsibilities, demands, and to-do list boxes to be checked off every single day. We're expected to work 9-to-5, hop on an important call, excel in our side hustle, pay the bills, fold the laundry that's been sitting in the dryer for two days, get dinner on the table, clean the house, wipe snotty noses, put the babies to bed, and sleep the recommended eight hours. The list goes on. In countless ways it feels like life demands every waking moment and every ounce of energy.

Truth be told, I haven't always felt so overwhelmed. I didn't always feel the weight of the world on my shoulders. I didn't always feel so overcome by my to-do list and my responsibilities that I cried at the kitchen sink.

But in that moment life was busier than it had ever been. I'd never felt more responsible or more needed. I was a wife. I was a new mom of the sweetest baby boy while also in the throes of postpartum depression and constant hormonal shifts. I was a brand-new author catapulted into the joys and complexities of publishing. I was a podcaster, social media content creator, daughter, and friend just trying to figure out how to juggle all of life's plates. Circumstances had shifted into high gear so quickly, and I couldn't keep up. "Overwhelmed," "overbooked," and "distracted" became my labels.

But what I experienced wasn't just a change of my daily routines but also a change in how I persevered and stayed present with Jesus. How was I supposed to live engaged in the fullness of my life and in my relationship with Jesus when I could barely think straight? How was I supposed to show up for Him and give Him all of me when I now had a tiny human to keep alive every moment of the day? My dreams were coming true, but they challenged everything I knew about putting Jesus first. Prioritizing the presence of God fell

Discover The Devoted Life

to the wayside when showing up to my new season was all I could manage or even think about.

Instead of stopping to question whether there was a root cause to all this frenzy, I kept doing, moving, and distracting myself. It was easier to be caught up by life's demands—and follow up by medicating with temporal entertainment and overbooking myself—than to stop and consider that maybe something was going on soul deep. Does that cycle sound familiar?

Chances are, you picked up this book because you're tired of that cycle. You can painfully relate to feeling both overbooked and overwhelmed. You aren't sure how to keep Jesus near when you are stretched so thin, and yet you long for a life free of constant burnout and soul exhaustion. It sounds like we're all looking for the same thing: We're looking for what Jesus calls "the abundant life" (John 10:10). But I wonder whether we've substituted the overcommitted life for that abundant life.

We all feel the tension: Life is full—not just of silly, inconsequential things but also of important things that God has placed in our laps. Some of us are wives, mothers, or students, while others are entrepreneurs, nurses, assistants, or ministry leaders. These are not bad responsibilities or opportunities. They're the good kingdom work and purpose God has given us. But where does spending intentional time with God fit into the hustle and bustle? How can we keep Him first when we're running at a breakneck pace, just trying to get through our days and get what needs to be done . . . done?

Overbooked and Overwhelmed

How do we keep Jesus first when our 9-to-5 feels more like 24-7? In a world where we have very real things to do each day, should we accept that this is just life?

A Full Life

During my sobbing-at-the-kitchen-sink era, whenever someone asked how I was doing or what I was up to, my default answer was "Life is full." Let's be honest. I probably even said those words in my sleep. I hoped people thought I was living a life of meaning and responsibility; I desperately wanted to prove that I was important and fulfilled, proudly wearing the label "stressed out for Jesus" as if it made me a holier Christian.

When I signed my publishing contract, I was three months pregnant. Six days before I birthed my son Hunter into the world, I hit Send on the first draft of my manuscript—all 58,000 words off to my editor. Three months postpartum I embarked on countless rounds of edits for said book. And on the same day that my son turned one, the finished product, *Surrender Your Story*, launched into the world. Sprinkle in parenting, working on my marriage, hosting people in our home, vacations, and a few other things.

Full, full, full. Life was brimming over.

But I was terrified to admit that I was sinking. Instead of surviving, I was drowning. I was riding the train to Burnout Station. I was stuffing down my problems and deprioritizing

Discover The Devoted Life

my relationship with God. Confronted with more responsibility and overwhelm than ever, I let Jesus become second place to busyness and duty. Spending time with Him was suddenly less urgent than getting important things done, hitting deadlines, and pumping out the productivity.

And then, because life just wouldn't stop, I decided the solution was to fill any free time I had with distractions. Instead of doing the thing that would lead to true soul satisfaction—seeking my Savior—I just kept cramming in anything that gave an immediate sense of happiness and relief. Television. Social media. Entertainment. Push the real problem down and keep going.

Life was full, that's for sure, but it was full of my own doing and of my desire for the wrong things.

Out of Focus

Everyone I know is busy. It's rare to have a conversation with someone that doesn't include what we got done in a day, our demanding schedules, and how strapped we all are. It's not just our feet that are running a million miles an hour; it's our brains too—pelted with thoughts ranging from what to make for dinner to how many minutes until bedtime.

My daily prayer used to be *God, give me more time to do* _____. I thought I needed more time to get things done, but in all reality, I needed more God. The problem was I had lost my focus.

Overbooked and Overwhelmed

One of my proudest achievements used to be my perfect eyesight, even though that's not even an achievement. Nearly half the people around me had glasses or contacts, so it was an odd point of pride for me to be lens-free. Until the day I sat nursing my newborn on the couch, covered in spit-up and days past my last shower. I glanced over to the kitchen to peek at the time on our microwave display, and the numbers were all fuzzy. I closed my eyes tight for a few seconds and then tried again. *Uh-oh*. I gulped.

At first I chalked up my blurry vision to sleepless nights, but my husband suggested I see an optometrist. After all, it had been a few years since my last visit. Reluctantly, I agreed—it couldn't hurt. A month later I walked out of my eye doctor's office with a pair of prescription glasses. My physical body was telling me that I needed help refocusing and seeing clearly. Ironically, my spiritual body was telling me that my relationship with God needed a similar reset.

God had never lost sight of me, but I had lost sight of Him in the hustle. My focus had changed because other shiny things had fallen into view and I couldn't seem to look away. The more I gazed on life's distractions and gave my time to everything but Him, the harder it was to see reality. My spiritual attention span was suffering.

A widely circulated statement, later shown to be false, claimed that research proved the average human has an attention span of 8.25 seconds. Even if that's not entirely true, the idea is staggering. But Netflix executives disagree with claims of lowering attention spans. From their team's internal research, they found that 73 percent of their platform's users had binge-watched a show—meaning, users had watched five or more hours of content in one single sitting.[1]

Each one of us makes thousands of choices a day, saying yes to some things and no to other things. We all get to decide what we give our attention to and, consequently, what we are not going to give our attention to. For the 73 percent of Netflix users who binge-watched a show, they made a choice to devote their time, energy, and focus to five hours of television.

In *The Ruthless Elimination of Hurry* John Mark Comer writes: "In the end, your life is no more than the sum of what you gave your attention to. That bodes well for those apprentices of Jesus who give the bulk of their attention to him and to all that is good, beautiful, and true in his world. But not for those who give their attention to the 24-7 news cycle of outrage and anxiety and emotion-charged drama or the nonstop feed of celebrity gossip, titillation, and cultural drivel."[2]

For better or for worse, what you give your attention to shapes who you become. Where your focus lies determines where you go. What you devote yourself to reveals the health of your heart.

Throughout this book you are going to hear me use the words "devoted" or "devotion" quite a bit. What do you think of when someone says, "He's devoted to his craft," or "She's devoted to her marriage," or "He's devoted to going to the gym every day"? You probably consider their work ethic. Their dedication to showing up. Their commitment to putting in the work to get better at what they do. Although their work and craft will have inevitable learning curves and struggles, although their marriages will go through hard and sticky seasons, although they will snooze their 5:00 a.m. alarm and skip the gym every now and then, they know the only way to the life they want is through devotion.

> *Mere desire to keep Jesus first without intention will get us only so far.*

Mere desire to keep Jesus first without intention will get us only so far. But wholehearted focus and devotion to Jesus will get us everywhere.

Before you quit your job, throw away your computer, and move into the woods thinking it's the solution to a less overwhelming life, let me just say this: Keeping up with Jesus doesn't mean you have to neglect the good and necessary responsibilities of life. The solution isn't praying on our knees for more time. It's more soul deep than that.

The solution is cultivating a devoted heart and consciously choosing not to let distraction win out. It's about reorienting and refocusing.

Reorientation is a change of direction. It's analyzing the ways in which we've been living, how they're affecting us, and turning to a new path. Refocusing is remembering, reprioritizing, and gaining perspective. And the first step is realizing we *need* to reorient and refocus.

Discover The Devoted Life

Breaking Point

A "breaking point" is "the point at which something loses force or validity."[3] It's the moment when a person or thing can no longer handle the stress or pressure of a situation and finally gives up. My breaking point, my wake-up call, was just the beginning. I wish I could tell you that it was like the flip of a switch—the difference between night and day. I wish I could tell you that from the moment I got honest with myself, I no longer struggled with a distracted heart. That I no longer pushed God or my Bible aside or let the world, social media, or achievement become worthier of my attention. But that's not how it happened.

Just months after I had launched *Surrender Your Story* into the world, there came a point when I finally felt like I could breathe. My jam-packed schedule of interviews, press, article writing, and content creation to promote the book was beginning to slow. For the first time in two years, I could hear myself think. I could hear the silence, but it was uncomfortable. I wasn't overbooked, and that terrified me.

It was a Monday, and my mom was babysitting Hunter. There—in that silence, in the haunting blank space of my planner—I sobbed. The moment I stopped running and stopped cramming, I realized the gaping hole in my soul. I realized that the noise and the constant exposure to distraction and stimulation were suffocating my relationship with God. I realized that it had been a few weeks since I'd opened my Bible and sat with Him there.

Overbooked and Overwhelmed

With tear-stained cheeks I reached for the Word that had grown dusty on my desk. I didn't really know where to turn, what to flip to, where to read. My fingers timidly dragged along the thin pages of my study Bible until I landed on some red letters: "For whoever would save his life will lose it, but whoever loses his life for my sake will find it" (Matthew 16:25).

Just moments after Jesus instructed His disciples in the Way—to die to themselves, take up their crosses, and follow Him—He proposed a thought-provoking question: "For what will it profit a man if he gains the whole world and forfeits his soul? Or what shall a man give in return for his soul?" (Matthew 16:26).

He knew the pull that the world would have on His followers. He knew that the accumulation of temporary wealth, accolades, and other such distractions would ultimately prove empty. Jesus loved His disciples so deeply that He wanted them to live abundant, undistracted, unhindered lives. And He wants the same for us.

The one who pursues their own will for their life will lose out in the end. And the one who puts everything else before God will also lose out in the end. Everything earthly that we protect, hold on to, or give our attention will be gone. But what remains? Who wins this thing called life? The one who sees their ultimate gain in Christ alone while simultaneously stewarding the good gifts in front of them. Jesus' words in Matthew 16 remind us that gaining the whole world—all the money, pleasure, and power of this life—offers no real, lasting benefit. Those things only pull our souls away from devoting our lives to what really matters.

If all of this feels overwhelming, let's take a minute to regroup. I see you, friend. I see how tired and overwhelmed you are by life. I see how overstimulated you are by the noise of things like your work, responsibilities, and social media. Your calendar is overbooked, and I bet you wonder when you're going to snap (maybe you already have). I see you discouraged, thinking that it isn't possible to keep Jesus first when your people, your work, and your to-do list require so much of you.

Quiet time? No way. The kids never stop talking.

Read the Bible every day? Have you seen my schedule?

Rest? I'll get to it when the laundry is clean, folded, and put away.

Sounds familiar, doesn't it? But I'm here to say that life doesn't have to just happen to you, whooshing past you in a frenzy. So often we accept that life is life. Overwhelming. Stressful. Busy. Overbooked. We shrug our shoulders and allow the demands to whisk us away—our energy, our time, and our affections. We accept that, in a world of social media, family responsibilities, work obligations, and extracurriculars, distracted and overstimulated *is* life. But it doesn't have to be. In the midst of it all, we can still walk by the Spirit. We can still be rooted, steady, and grounded by devoting ourselves to Jesus as our foundation.

Overbooked and Overwhelmed

In Christ You Are Complete

I rarely remember my dreams when I wake up in the morning, but I remember one particular dream so vividly. It was like I was in *A Christmas Carol*, the novel about Scrooge and the ghosts of Christmas past, present, and future who show Scrooge different possible outcomes of his life. In my dream I hovered above my own life just like Scrooge, and what I saw made my stomach turn. That Tara down below was so overwhelmed by life that she was frantic. That Tara was so pulled apart that she was snapping at her husband, exhausted from a lack of sleep, dangerously close to a mental breakdown, verging on depression and anxiety, and spiritually shriveling away. That Tara was succumbing to the distractions around her and ignoring her relationship with God.

As silly as that all sounds, God used my dream to point out something uncomfortable: That dream-Tara looked an awful lot like the real-world-Tara.

Remember those three little words from earlier? "Life is full"? I've discovered something incredible about the dictionary's definition of the word "full." Like most words, "full" has more than one definition.

1. having no empty space[4]
2. abundant; well-supplied[5]

Wait. Read that again.
The word "full" has two very different definitions. When

I realized that, it made me pause and wonder. *Which definition of "full" do I want to be living?*

If we want complete lives, we can't live without space for Jesus. If we want lives of abundance and not lack, we can't live strung out. If we want the wildly wonderful, purpose-filled life that Jesus died for, we must give Him our devotion. We must give Him first place. Sound impossible? I'm here to say it doesn't have to be. But don't just take my word for it. Come along with me and take *the* Word for it.

If you want to live complete in Christ and discover practical, life-giving ways to juggle your distractions and responsibilities while keeping Jesus first, you're in the right place.

If you're tired of feeling too overstimulated and overwhelmed by life to sit in the presence of God, you're in the right place.

If you want to learn how to retrain your cravings and desire God more than the world, you're in the right place.

If you want to learn how to resist hustle culture, avoid burnout, fight spiritual fatigue, sit in the presence of God, find true rest in Him, and run your race for Him rooted in your identity, you're in the right place.

This certainly isn't a book about living in radical extremes, because life has too much nuance for that. But it *is* a book about living radically in love with God first. So let's get off the culture ride. It's time to reclaim what is ours—a sound mind and heart.

Jesus is the steady heartbeat of our lives that keeps us

If we want complete lives, we can't live without space for Jesus.

grounded, sane, and connected even when our lives are full to the max. You can start living devoted rather than distracted today. Yes, even if it feels like all you have to offer Him is your meager margin. Even if you feel a little crazy, a little frantic, and—dare I say—a little unhinged. Spoiler alert: That's the perfect place to start.

Reflection Questions

1. What is your life "full" of? Identify a few of your top responsibilities. What fills your weekly calendar? Write them down as we start this journey.
2. What causes you to feel the most overwhelmed? Confess those things to God and begin to surrender them to Him in prayer.
3. How can you devote yourself to God and to growing your relationship with Him this week? Start small, maybe even with just a few minutes set aside with your Bible and a cup of coffee tomorrow morning.

TWO

The Cost of Distraction

No love of the natural heart is safe unless the human heart has been satisfied by God first.
OSWALD CHAMBERS

*M*any of us have those nights. You know, hair-wash nights. You either love them or hate them. It's either your self-care night or a dreaded night that never ends. And sometimes you even have a designated day of the week for it. Mine is usually Thursday. Now, I have a lot of hair and it's thick—so thick that my mom named it the "horse's mane" after years of wrangling it into a ballet bun. So, on Thursday nights, after we put Hunter down for bed, I embark on the near hourlong process. First, I double wash with a purple shampoo to tone my balayage color, and then I apply a leave-in conditioner, wash my body, and shave, then blow-dry the horse's mane.

One night, I had an epiphany in the shower during hair-wash night. Some of my most important thoughts—like what we need to restock and put on our grocery list or what scripture I should reference for this book—come to me in the shower. As I stood waiting for my hair masque to do its thing, my eyes drifted to the back of my bodywash bottle. The text on the bottle went something like this: "Enjoy this relaxing combination of eucalyptus, rosewater, and other botanicals. This calming bodywash will wipe away the anxiety of your day. Lather all over and escape from it all."

Call it what you will—clever marketing jargon or harmless rhetoric—but I couldn't help but laugh as I rinsed out my masque. Even our bodywash bottles are claiming to

Overbooked and Overwhelmed

have the solution to our stress, overwhelm, and jam-packed schedules.

Stressed? Lather in rose botanicals.

Overwhelmed? Breathe deep the eucalyptus scent.

Craving relief from the struggles and burdens of life? Take a nice, long self-care shower and forget what's bringing you down.

We are pushed products and services every day that promise to change our lives, cure our every ailment, and solve our problems. Personal-development books dominate bestseller lists. Self-help and self-care podcasts reach millions of downloads every year. Products are advertised as "must-haves." I'll be the first to admit that those marketing efforts catch my eye.

I once stumbled upon a YouTube video by an influencer who lives in New York documenting her typical work-from-home day. As I wiped off my makeup and got ready for bed, I hit Play. Halfway through the video she shared how pink noise had changed her life. Apparently, white noise is so out and pink and brown noise are so in (I'm still not even sure what brown noise is). She shared how overbooked and overwhelmed she was and how her Spotify pink-noise playlist was the cure, a means to occupy her mind with something other than the worries and troubles of life.

I thought skeptically, *Wow, she thinks that's going to make a difference? She thinks that's going to cure her stress?*

But as I lathered on my moisturizer, I realized that I was like the girl I was judging so harshly. I wasn't listening to

The Cost of Distraction

pink noise to calm my anxious mind, but I, too, was using life's daily distractions to shut out the noise. I was lamenting how hard life was but hadn't considered trading in distraction for devotion to God. I had convinced myself that filling my mind with noise was calming, multitasking was the only way to survive, and overworking and overbooking were holy. Was that really any different from trusting in bodywash or pink noise to cure your stress? And where has all this self-medicating gotten us?

Well, if you're like me, you've become so overwhelmed that you cry every single day. You feel like you constantly have to keep up with the flow of culture and then wonder why you struggle to keep your attention on the one thing that matters most. We all want to get well, but we've made ourselves our own physicians—and we're lousy at recommending the right prescriptions. We prescribe vice after vice, distraction after distraction, in pursuit of wholeness. We search for answers online from people who have similar experiences, only to be left still lacking. At some point we need to admit that we need a better Physician.

Now, hear me out. Before we go any further, I need you to know this: There is nothing inherently wrong with enjoying the comforts, pleasures, and gifts of life. There's nothing inherently sinful about being a Christian and engaging online. But we must be careful not to let each little comfort and pleasure take our eyes off Jesus, the Best Thing, or let them become more important to us than He is. The world does not own our hearts and minds. So it's time we reclaim what is ours in Christ.

True Soul Satisfaction

In Judges 13 we're introduced to a hunky man of God named Samson, with luscious hair and the strength to tear a lion to pieces. Pretty much what any Christian girl is looking for, right? Well, you may be surprised to learn that, although Samson was such a biblical heartthrob, his story is ultimately one of distraction.

In ancient Israel, leaders—or judges, as they were called—were handpicked by God to deliver the Israelites from their enemies. Think of them as military leaders who executed God's will through conquering cities, bringing down corrupt kings, prophesying, and riding lots of donkeys (true story). Samson was one of God's chosen judges, born a miracle from a mother who was barren. As a symbol of his consecration to God and his calling to bring down the Philistines, one of Israel's fiercest enemies, Samson was to never cut his luscious locks. From the moment he entered the world, he had an incredible anointing from God on his life.

But Samson lost focus. Something shiny caught his eye: a beautiful Philistine woman. Yes, a woman who was part of

The Cost of Distraction

the tribe that Samson was raised to defeat. Then, after conquering the Philistines, Samson shacked up with Delilah, another Philistine woman; this time a prostitute.[1] This story doesn't have a fairy-tale ending. It reads more like a horror story, culminating in betrayal and death. Ultimately, Samson allowed Delilah to steal his God-given strength and purpose, cutting his consecrated hair and tricking him into being captured by the Philistines.

Judges 16:20 says, "But he [Samson] did not know that the LORD had left him." He assumed all the way down the road of sin and distraction that the Lord was with him. But Samson had so far removed himself from relationship with God and allowed lust to distract him that he was oblivious when the Lord quietly departed from him.

Distraction has a cost. At first it feels harmless and exciting and pleasurable. But if we journey down its road for too long, we'll find ourselves at a dead end. The temptation will be to camp out at the end of the road, zipping ourselves up and blocking out the problem, because getting serious about our distractions might require serious energy. But dealing with the long-term consequences of letting distractions win over and over again takes far more time than confronting them, reorienting with God, and admitting to Him what overwhelms us. Distraction has a way of sweeping us up, up, and away from reality. It disconnects us from reality. And as followers of Christ, our lives really matter. They matter now, and they matter for eternity.

I don't want you to forget: You have an important role

to play in God's kingdom. You have a purposeful mission to live out each day. You have assignments, callings, gifts, and responsibilities to steward. You are needed by so many to show up and shine the light of Christ. While there are parts of life we can't escape, there are also many parts we willingly volunteer to be overwhelmed by, distractions we choose to soothe our overwhelm that end up adding to it instead.

I would guess that Samson's calling weighed heavily on him at times. And it probably felt soothing to find rest and pleasure in the arms of the Philistine women. But the comfort of distractions never lasts, and the consequences of distractions are serious.

Think about it: Working distracted makes us less productive. Driving distracted makes us dangerous. Studying distracted makes us less likely to do well on a test. Scrolling distracted while talking to our spouses makes us inattentive and, dare I say, disrespectful. Cooking distracted makes us prone to burning or overseasoning our food beyond repair. And living spiritually distracted for a sustained period makes our souls suffer.

Instead of letting ourselves be lulled into complacency, we need to put up a fight. We need to change our minds and hearts—and thus our actions—and the first step in doing that is acknowledging a disconnect between us and Jesus, a distraction that is coming between that relationship. Can you name one thing that has diminished your ability to keep in step with Jesus? Disconnects or distractions can come in a variety of forms:

The Cost of Distraction

- social media (Instagram, TikTok, YouTube, and more)
- possessions (cars, clothes, products)
- money and finances
- the pursuit of fame
- comparison
- pornography
- family or relationships (Yes, even good things can distract us!)
- television
- work
- school
- world news
- daily anxieties and worries
- sin

Now that we've named our distractions, the second step is getting real and honest in our hearts. After mentally acknowledging what has created a disconnect between us and our heavenly Father, we have to address the heart—or, as Proverbs puts it, our true motivator. This step requires not only asking ourselves a sincere question but giving a sincere answer.

The question: *Do you like being distracted?* Your answer will make all the difference.

Friend, I'm not going to sugarcoat it for you. Distraction brought me a *crazy* level of comfort and happiness. Bingeing *Gilmore Girls* for three hours after Hunter went to bed was my "me" time. Watching hilarious Instagram reels and admiring other people's aesthetic lives for hours on end entertained me like nothing else. Each pleasure met me with comfort, relaxation, and an escape when life was more than I could handle.

But this is where it gets sticky. If we're being honest, a lot of us don't see distraction as a detriment to our souls. We don't see the problem. Don't we deserve to enjoy what makes us feel happy and rested? Don't we deserve a little relief and entertainment when we work hard or when life is hard? Is distraction really that soul deep? What if it's just the norm in this thing we call the twenty-first century?

I've said it once and I'll say it again: There's nothing inherently sinful about enjoying your life. After all, God gave you this life! He didn't create you for a flat, boring, one-dimensional existence. He created you for a full-color, multidimensional life—one He longs for you to enjoy in its fullness, with all His good creation. But are those things distracting you from what you were created for first and foremost?

Intimate attachment to God.

Wholehearted devotion to God.

Relationship and friendship with God.

I don't know about you, but I don't want to have a Samson ending of my own. I don't want to look back and realize I was pulled in every direction except toward God. I don't want to find that my view of God was fuzzy and out of focus the whole time, while the temporal things of life were crystal clear.

The Cost of Distraction

I'm not here to tell you to quit your job, stop taking care of your family, throw in the towel at school, or sit on your hands until Jesus comes again. What I am saying is that not only is it possible to keep up with God and keep Him first, even when life is busy and distracting, but it's a blessing. A blessing worth chasing time and time again, no matter how often we've messed up or lost focus.

Devotion is how we were knit together. Attachment to the Word Himself, not the world, is how we were created to thrive. When we live in the way that God created us, we find rest. We find comfort. We find satisfaction. No matter how many storms, struggles, and temptations arise, when we follow the path our Good Shepherd desires to lead us on, we will never be left wanting. We will always be fully satisfied.

Netflix and Instagram may provide a hit of dopamine or a retreat from reality, and they definitely have their perks, but those perks are fleeting for our souls. A well that will always run out, a cistern too broken to hold anything of value. But how our souls really, truly, and deeply find satisfaction is through devoting ourselves to God.

You Are a Whole Person

At month three postpartum I started back to my part-time work of podcasting, writing, and ministry. Then the dreaded mom guilt I had feared reared its ugly head. No one can really prepare you for the emotional pendulum swings of being away from your baby. The joy you feel getting back into a job you love. The sadness you feel as you miss your baby's sweet snuggles. The excitement you experience when you feel even a little bit more like yourself. The sting of guilt when you think of someone else caring for your child. Talk about a roller coaster of emotions.

In the thick of those first few weeks back at my desk, I reached out in desperation to a working-mom friend of mine. I asked her if it was always going to feel this way. Although I was only away from my boy for a few hours each week, the guilt was all consuming.

My friend replied gently, "Tara, you know that God made you a *whole* person, right?"

She was talking about the fact that, however indescribably wonderful motherhood was, it was not my identity. In Christ, I find my identity. Motherhood is not what makes me whole. My Savior has made me whole.

Friend, the reality is, we are fragmented people when our hearts are distracted. To be distracted is to be torn apart, absent-minded, frenzied, distraught, distressed, and panicked. When our sights are set on the world instead of fixed on the Word, we shouldn't be surprised when we feel overwhelmed and as though something is missing.

One person who knew exactly what this felt like was King Solomon. He was among the few who had it all—every flashy thing he could buy or take or own was his, every pleasure and every form of entertainment available at the snap of his fingers. But, as we read in Ecclesiastes, the book scholars speculate he wrote, he came not only to the end of his life but to the end of himself: "I kept my heart from no pleasure, for my heart found pleasure in all my toil, and this was my reward for all my toil. Then I considered all that my hands had done and the toil I had expended in doing it, and behold, all was vanity and striving after wind, and there was nothing to be gained under the sun" (Ecclesiastes 2:10–11).

Solomon was a man who had everything at his fingertips. I would bet that he admitted to being distracted many times in his life—distracted by building mansions, securing slaves, raising the finest livestock, hosting the best parties, accumulating gold, and meeting all the women he could ever want. But what was his conclusion at the end of it all? It was all a vapor, a fleeting thought, not anything that would truly satisfy. In Ecclesiastes 3:11 he wrote, "He [God] has put eternity into man's heart." All our striving and our craving as we jump from one thing to the next, it's all just us searching for something lasting, something eternal: a satisfaction far beyond this life and its distractions. The things of God. Attachment to God.

Ecclesiastes 3 is a beautiful foreshadowing of the coming Savior who would hang on a tree for us. Jesus' death, burial, and resurrection were about wholeness. He died to seal up the God-shaped hole in each of our hearts, to restore the relationship that was severed in the garden of Eden when Adam and Eve chose their own desires over their relationship with God. Sin had fractured not only who we were as individuals but also our communion with God. Our restless souls have been

Overbooked and Overwhelmed

wandering around, searching and longing, ever since Eden. But the night our Savior was born, He brought an end to the fracture, a solution to the longing, an answer for our restless souls. Jesus conquered sin to bring His light to the world, giving us new hearts able to fix on Him.

In Christ you are a whole person with a whole mind. No matter the brokenness of this world or how broken our physical frames may feel, the reality is that in Christ we are new. We are whole. Those who trust in God lack no good thing. As Jesus breathed His last and fulfilled His mission on earth, He cried, "*Tetelestai!*" ("It is finished!"), signaling the end to and completion of His saving work. But not just any kind of end. A successful end. A once-and-for-all end. An entirely perfect finale. Sin was defeated, wholeness was ushered in, and the path to eternity fixed forever. It was finished in the past, it is finished in the present, and it will be finished forever.

I love the way *The Message* version of 1 Thessalonians 5 talks about this transformation: "May God Himself, the God who makes everything holy and whole, make you holy and whole, put you together—spirit, soul, and body—and keep you fit for the coming of our Master, Jesus Christ. The One who called you is completely dependable. If he said it, he'll do it!" (vv. 23–24).

Your heavenly Father is wholly, completely, and undeniably committed to you and your growth. He is 1,000 percent committed to seeing you through, from the moment you were born to the moment you meet Him face-to-face in heaven.

He is the God who stays when everyone else walks away and when everything else fades away. He is the God who never takes His eyes off you. He is the God who is wholeheartedly devoted to you.

I know the distraction is real. I know the comfort found in numbing out and checking out feels good. I know it seems harmless and meaningless. But it all adds up. I think we often look at the most beautiful flower fields or the grandest oak trees and marvel at their beauty. We wonder how they got there. Any good farmer will tell you that growth happens little by little. Moment by moment. The day you plant the seed isn't the day you see the bloom. A healthy and lasting root system must first grow down deep and then branch outward. Roots that grow deep and wide provide stability, setting that plant on a course toward establishment. Immovability. And as the plant is continually watered and fertilized, its growth only solidifies. The same goes for you and me. The little choices we make each day, saying yes to either devotion or distraction, add up. Our choices, like ignoring our Bible yet again and scrolling social media, may feel inconsequential in the moment, but those choices put down roots, too, whether we realize it or not.

Get Up out of That Grave

I've lost count of how many seasons of my life have felt like scenes from *The Walking Dead*. I've lost count of how many

The *little choices* we make each day, saying yes to either devotion or distraction, *add up*

The Cost of Distraction

times I've merely shuffled through life, pulled apart, dragged apart, and certainly not set apart. But I'm done with that. God didn't create you and me to merely stumble our way through life. To just get by, hanging by a thread, pulling ourselves apart at the seams. God created us to live fully awake to new life in Jesus Christ.

Romans 6:4 says, "We were buried therefore with him by baptism into death, in order that, just as Christ was raised from the dead by the glory of the Father, we too might walk in the newness of life." Did you catch that? We were saved to walk in newness. Saved to walk in life. Saved to get up out of that grave.

But I wonder, How many of us are allowing life to keep us buried? How many of us are letting the enemy keep us stuck in that grave? How many of us are rolling over and allowing our burdens to weigh us down?

Jennie Allen wrote, "What we believe and what we think about matters, and the enemy knows it. And he is determined to get in your head to distract you from doing good and to sink you so deep that you feel helpless, overwhelmed, shut down, and incapable of rising to make a difference for the kingdom of God."[2]

This was exactly what I had allowed the enemy to do in my life. And do you know what the crazy thing was? Ever since I was a little kid, my parents had considered me a confrontational, say-whatever-you're-thinking kind of kid. I wasn't about to be pushed around. I didn't mince words, and I didn't back down from a fight. But it was a completely different story when it came to confronting my own sin and not letting it or the enemy call the shots.

At first distraction was a disease that I didn't want to address. I didn't want to uncover it or bring it to light for fear of being left vulnerable—naked, bare, and honest. I worried that confronting my overwhelmed soul with the truth of God's Word would remove all security—or what I thought was security. Sound familiar? Sometimes we wonder whether choosing Jesus over everything else might make things more complicated, hard, and uncomfortable. So we keep ourselves busy. We keep ourselves occupied. We wall ourselves off from God, because if we let Him in, that might just wreck the castles of sand we've been building. So, instead, we keep filling our lives with things.

Taking that first, tender step to come face-to-face with my sin and shortcomings was nothing short of terrifying. Admitting that I had let God slip through the cracks and had struggled to keep up with Him unearthed guilt, shame, and regret. But as I came to realize, and as I need you to realize today, that shame is from the enemy, and shame does not win the game. Like Jennie said, the enemy is a determined little devil. Don't let him take advantage of the guilt you feel from your past choices and discourage you from moving forward. Jesus is greater than the one who lives in the world. He does not say, "Shame on you for allowing yourself to be distracted and displaced from Me."

Instead Jesus says, "Come to me . . . for I am gentle and lowly in heart" (Matthew 11:28–29).

The Cost of Distraction

If the shame, regret, or guilt from not keeping Jesus first is holding you back from living devoted, I'm here to tell you that you can start again. You can start today. You can start now. You can be fully present in the life God has given you, even when life doesn't slow down. He makes a way where there seems to be no possible way for you to do this.

God has created you for a devoted life—two feet planted, eyes focused, heart set with purpose—regardless of how overwhelmed or overbooked you feel. Onward.

Reflection Questions

1. What things distract you the most from giving your time and attention to Jesus?
2. Where do you tend to turn for rest and refreshment when life is hard?
3. Be honest with yourself and God in this moment. Have you been allowing shame or other strongholds from the enemy to keep you from addressing your heart condition?

THREE

Identify Your Cravings

When you binge-eat or light up or browse social media, what you really want is not a potato chip or a cigarette or a bunch of likes. What you really want is to feel different.

JAMES CLEAR

I haven't always had the best relationship with food, and it all started with ballet class.

When I was four, my parents took me to my very first dance class. After that, I was hooked. The baby-pink tights, a cap-sleeve leotard, those silky wrap skirts, and the soft ballet shoes. I was *in*. Dance in all forms—ballet, jazz, contemporary—was the air I breathed. Pointe shoes, jazz leggings, and bobby pins. For fourteen years, multiple days a week, you would find me in the dance studio, covered in sweat, rosin, and sometimes tears.

My ballet teacher once told me that she noticed a special spark in me from the beginning. I had a rare drive, determination, and competitiveness for such a young girl. Now that I've stopped dancing, I'm slightly horrified at how intense I was at four years old. I scolded and shushed the other girls in my class who messed up their footwork, goofed off, or were not listening to the teacher. I'm happy to report that I lightened up as the years went by, but that intensity was four-year-old Tara's way of showing just how much she loved to dance and just how meaningful it was to her.

In those early years, I never cared a stitch about how my body looked in a leotard and tights. I never thought that I looked chubby or that something was wrong with my appearance. I never questioned whether or not I had the quintessential ballet body, which truthfully I didn't. But something changed in my teen years. I started calling out all the things that were "wrong" with my body. I didn't have the long legs and lines like my peers. I had a broad rib cage and muscular arms, whereas my friends had narrower chests and slender, feminine arms. Instead of showing up to dance freely and unashamed, I started to wear black leggings over my leotards, hoping it would make me look slimmer, that it would cover up all the flaws that I saw, so that no one else would see them too.

That shame wasn't isolated to the dance studio. It followed me home. Eating became a mind game. I jumped through mental hoops to earn my calories and made insane calculations to justify every bite. You can imagine how hungry I was after a three-hour dance class, right? How many calories I had burned and how dearly my body needed fuel? Well, after eating a healthy dinner, I would look down at my empty plate with self-loathing. I would slip on my metaphorical boxing gloves and beat myself up for eating what I thought was too much. Worry consumed me. I wondered, *What am I going to look like in my leotard after eating that dinner?* Hit. *That pasta and the handful of chips I just ate—is it going to show in my midsection?* Hit. *I need to work extra hard tomorrow in class to make up for that meal.* Knockout.

But it wasn't all self-loathing and restrictive eating. At various points in my life, I slipped into short seasons of binge eating. Food was a comfort when my fibromyalgia was especially trying. Food was a satisfying companion when I dropped out of college, moved home, and felt completely hopeless and directionless. Food was a distraction that fulfilled a temporary desire to just escape it all. After sustained seasons of eating to excess, my body was trained to eat with little restraint. The longer this went on, the more I fed and trained my addiction. What I realize now is that my cravings for food weren't just about food. They were tied to situations and stressors.

Perhaps you have struggled to find a healthy relationship with food too. No matter your struggles, I think we can all agree that the root of an unhealthy relationship with food is usually deeper than food itself. Here's what I mean. When I restricted myself, I craved a "perfect" body. When I punished myself for eating too much, I craved a likable self-image to display to others. When I binge ate a bag of potato chips and a few bowls of ice cream in one sitting, I craved a comfort and satisfaction that I thought would last. But really it was yet another way to distract me from how stressful and overwhelming life was.

You might be wondering how cravings fit into distractions and overwhelm. Well, here's why we need an entire chapter on this: Our cravings have been affected by the fall. Even when we've given our lives to Jesus and received a regenerated spirit through Him, we still wrestle day-to-day with our flesh. The apostle Paul tells us that we still struggle with our "old self," the old ways in which we used to live before we met Jesus (Ephesians 4:22). That means we must expect a fight. We must be prepared to meet anything that tries to take our first love away from Christ.

What we crave, or what we desire, influences the way we live. What we value most in this life is what we give most of our time and attention to. This isn't to say that craving something is inherently evil. But if cravings are left unchecked or are unhealthy, these desires can harm our souls. If we're not aware of what we consume, we may just become the ones consumed.

When we crave and value other things above God, we lose perspective. But we're called to value and desire God first and to let that first love influence the way we work, mother, serve—the way we live our lives. When we allow our souls to become so cluttered and noisy to the point of missing Jesus in the everyday, that's a surefire sign that our value system is off.

When our life inventory is overflowing with distractions, we need to put in the work to do a spiritual deep clean. I know it's easier and more comfortable not to disrupt the flow, nuances, or circumstances of life, but in order to be holy, we also need to be honest.

What Do You Crave?

Mere months into our marriage, I found out I was pregnant. And four months after that, we found out that we were having a baby boy. An old wives' tale says that if you're having

Identify Your Cravings

a girl, you crave sweet, and if you're having a boy, you crave salty. This was spot-on for me. During the first trimester, Sprite, saltine crackers, and vitamin B6 were practically the only things my somersaulting stomach could handle. But as soon as my nausea halted in the second trimester, I craved Top Ramen and Cheetos like nobody's business.

My cravings were relatively tame compared to some of the wild stories I've heard—one of the craziest stories being a craving for dirt. Yes, you heard me. Dirt. For the longest time I was convinced that this couldn't be true, until I did some research. Doctors call the phenomenon of craving items that aren't food "pica." Although it remains somewhat of a mystery, health professionals claim that these unusual cravings are linked to anemia, a deficiency of red blood cells. It's not uncommon for expectant mothers to have anemia; after all, the body is working overtime to create a surplus of blood in support of the life growing in her belly.[1]

My point? It's not that these women think that dirt is downright delicious. It's that their bodies are telling them that something is missing. Dirt contains a substantial amount of iron, which is a supplement that doctors prescribe to people with anemia. What's happening with this kind of pica is a desire for something to satisfy a natural deficiency. I'm sure you would agree with me when I say that I, too, have a deep desire for something to satisfy a deficiency in my soul.

Our souls have deep, important needs. We long for peace, comfort, security, and acceptance. So what do we do with that longing? Naturally, we go in search of anything that might satisfy those needs or might feel good: Social media. Food. Romantic relationships. Affirmation. Accomplishment. Money. Work. Entertainment. Sleep. Busyness. And yet soul needs do not have superficial remedies. Soul needs require supernatural resources that only Christ can give.

Follow ~~Your Heart~~ Jesus

Ezekiel 11 contains one of the most well-known verses about our hearts: "I will give them an undivided heart and put a new spirit in them; I will remove from them their heart of stone and give them a heart of flesh" (v. 19 NIV). Ouch, God. My stony, stubborn heart? That verse used to feel like a diss, not so much like an encouragement—that is, until I realized it was true. This verse isn't a slam on me, nor is it violently graphic, but it is actually loving and gracious.

Before Jesus, people lived by what is called the old covenant. It was given to God's people as their law, meant to work from the outside in. This passage foreshadowed what was to come: God's promise for a new covenant. A renewing that would work from the inside out, addressing the deeper soul issues that external acts, like animal sacrifices, couldn't cover.

Someone with a heart of stone acts in defiance, inflexibility, stubbornness; but a heart of flesh, softened by the truth of God's Word, lives in submission, tenderness, and receptivity to Christ, however imperfectly. The Spirit of God cannot

Identify Your Cravings

dwell in the old, stony heart. That's why, when we choose to follow Jesus, God's first operation is to pull down the old house and build Himself a new one.

Think about this with me for a moment: Your heart was mirrored after God's own heart.[2] God created you in His image. The road map, model, mold that He created our hearts from was His own. This is our good design. But free will tends to mess with that design. Some people who are against Christianity suppose that God is no more than a senseless dictator or a loveless slave driver who wants to create robotic minions. But our loving God gives us a choice. From the beginning of time, starting with Adam and Eve, He gave us the choice of how to live, move, and be (Acts 17:28). Because what would a true and loving relationship be without the choice to have it? Kidnapping and coercion are not God's methods of creating devoted disciples. Love, free will, and forgiveness are.

That's why God sent Jesus into the world. To bring the words of Ezekiel, and many others, into full focus. Just as you and I do, the Israelites needed a visit to their heavenly Eye Doctor, the One who would bring them back into focus and illuminate what really mattered. Those who chose Jesus and chose life would receive a new, regenerated heart. It wasn't about ultimatums but about a loving, beckoning call to choose Him, because He was and is better than anything the world offers.

Consider the lyrics to one of my favorite hymns, "Turn Your Eyes upon Jesus":

> Turn your eyes upon Jesus,
> Look full in His wonderful face,
> And the things of earth will grow
> > strangely dim,
> In the light of His glory and grace.

The author of this hymn, Helen Lemmel, didn't say that the things of earth would disappear. She didn't say that when we look at Jesus, the distractions and desires of this world wouldn't be tempting, nor did she say that we shouldn't enjoy His good gifts. What she *did* say was that when we turn to take Jesus in, in all His fullness, His glory will prove to be greater than anything else.

Don't Lose Heart

Can you feel it? Can you see it? A wind of change, a tide of transformation turning and churning, your heart yearning to say yes. I feel it too. Perhaps you've tried to be your own heart surgeon. You've tried to change your ways, make Jesus the priority of your heart, keep up and keep Him first, but you keep falling short. Nothing seems to last, nothing seems to stick, and you feel caught on a merry-go-round of unchanging patterns.

The heart is a fickle thing, which is what makes this good news: God is the One who does the heart work. He is the only one powerful enough to change us, revive us,

Identify Your Cravings

and realign us. He is the One with a never-ending supply of grace. Dane Ortlund said, "Divine grace is so radical that it reaches down and turns around our very desires. Our eyes are open. Christ becomes beautiful. We come to him. And anyone is . . . welcome."[3]

Isn't it a relief that this tender and transformative work isn't up to us? Take hope in the fact that God sees your heart and knows your desires. He knows that, although it's hard and exhausting, you want to desire Him more than anything and you want to live devoted to Him, not distracted by your cravings. God hasn't stopped working on your heart, and He never will. That inner work is often hard to see, but it is there. But that doesn't mean we sit on our hands and just wait around for something to change. We roll up our sleeves and participate in the work God starts and sustains in us.

Women of faith don't take the enemy's attacks or the allures of the world lying down. With grit and strength, they stand up and fight. They put themselves in the position to be needy, to be hungry, and to be receptive. They drag their hearts along, even if they're sluggish, even if they're kicking and screaming, even if all they can drag along feels like a tiny sliver (God loves that offering too), asking the Lord to grow their desires. To grow their cravings to thirst for more of Him and less of the world. Even if their fight feels feeble, they trust that when God says He is their strength, He means it.

What does that look like in the day-to-day? Here are a few methods you might use to stand up as a woman of faith and grit today.

God is the one who does the *heart work.* He is the only one powerful enough to *change us, revive us, and realign us*

Identify Your Cravings

SUBMIT EVERYTHING TO GOD.

The word "submit" is used in a variety of ways, one of which is as a military term, illustrating the idea of arranging troops in a tactical fashion under the command of a leader. Now think of "submit" in terms of your relationship with God. Submitting your life to God is giving everything over to Him in obedience. It's trusting your life and all it entails to a God who has an eternal viewpoint. When we grasp the reality that all life is God's and that everything we have is from His hand, we're able to live in openhanded surrender and submission. If everything is God's anyway, then what's the point of holding on to it so tightly?

Practically, this looks like taking captive our thoughts and our actions and surrendering them in prayer to God every day. Say you are struggling with wanting screen time more than face time with God in His Word. Ask the Father to help you submit your screen time to Him so that you can be obedient to the Word instead.

ANALYZE YOUR ENVIRONMENT.

When I realized just how deeply overwhelmed I was, I also realized how lazy I had gotten in my daily rhythms and routines. There was hardly anything in my day-to-day routine that was encouraging a healthy and holy relationship with God. One of the first practical steps I took was evaluating my environment.

I wasn't reading my Bible every day. Heck, I was barely reading it once a week. My Bible lived in my office, just to the left of my desktop. As I studied my routine, I noticed that every time I sat down with the intention to read God's Word, I immediately got distracted by the dozens of emails, deadlines, and notifications blinking across my screen. When I moved my Bible, notebook, and pens out of my office and into my bedroom, everything changed.

Adjusting your environment may be a helpful first step for you too. Try moving your iPad or phone out of your bedroom. Or try scattering truth in your most frequented places in your home using sticky notes.

CONSUME WHAT IS GOOD FOR YOU, NOT JUST WHAT FEELS GOOD IN THE MOMENT.

My husband decided to cut back on his sugar intake a few years ago after noticing the negative effects it was having on his body. I think he believed it would be easier to stop eating sugar altogether than it actually was. For the first few weeks, he had the most intense cravings for it. His body was withdrawing, missing the sugary goodness it was used to consuming. He would be the first to tell you that it was hard, but one thing that helped drastically was replacing refined sugar with more protein and whole foods. Although steak and apple slices don't have the same taste as a piece of candy, over time he began to enjoy the food he was eating. Michael was consuming what was good for his body (with a few inevitable cheat days sprinkled in), and the more he consistently did that, the better he felt. He even had more energy. The same goes for retraining our cravings to hunger after God first.

We need to consume what is spiritually healthy and good and right for us. We can't neglect our soul's truest need: time with God in prayer and in the Word. We must feast in His presence daily, even if just for a few minutes. You will reap the benefits of consuming the right things. That is a guarantee.

GO SLOWLY, GO SIMPLY, AND DON'T FORGET TO ENJOY.

Although I'm a natural-born planner, sometimes I get so excited about an idea, dream, or business plan that I jump in headfirst without thinking. Straight into the deep end I go. What usually happens, though, is that I falter, sputter, and start to drown because I put too much on my plate at once. When we're trying to reclaim our attention span and put it back on Christ, we need to give ourselves the grace to go slowly and go simply. There isn't a quick fix. Reclaiming our attention is a slow and steady journey of learning to live in the world and in the world's distractions but not be *of* them. That's why we need to be realistic.

If your desire is to be less distracted by social media because you've been using it for six-plus hours a day, it's likely not doable for you to quit it cold turkey tomorrow. If you desire to be more present with God, it's likely not doable (or right) for you to stop taking care of your family, doing the laundry, or washing the dishes. If you desire to be less overwhelmed by your to-do list, it's likely not doable to get rid of that list and your responsibilities altogether.

Just as when we're trying to make any other change in

our lives, the key is to start small and go slowly, instead of jumping immediately to extremes. For example, a strict food diet isn't usually sustainable for a lifetime, and cheat days aren't unhealthy—they're actually encouraged by most fitness trainers. Depriving your body completely of Doritos or never allowing yourself to have a milkshake is not viable and, quite frankly, a bit legalistic. As you walk this path toward keeping Jesus first, allow yourself to enjoy the pleasures of this world; just be careful not to let them consume you.

FIND YOUR PEOPLE.

Who inspires you to live devoted? Who is someone who has an admirable relationship with God? Get in rooms with those people. Buy them a cup of coffee. Learn from them. Figure out what success in their relationship with God looks like. Find out their routines and rhythms, remembering that they are imperfect just like you and me. Then borrow the practices that work for you.

Take it a step further and set up a support system for yourself. Accountability has never come easy for me. For a long time, I rarely asked people to check in on me or help me progress through struggles. This was a result of the sin of pride keeping me from vulnerability and honesty with others and, in turn, with Christ. It was easier to let people think I had it all together and not share the ways in which I wanted to grow, because if I messed up, God forbid, they would know about it. And they might even call me out and call me higher to a holier standard of living. But if we're serious about getting devoted to God and not letting distractions enslave us, then we have to be people who rely on other godly people. By finding the right brothers and sisters in Christ—the ones who are loving, understanding, empathetic, but also challenging—we'll be steps closer to reclaiming our eternal focus and handling the overwhelm of life.

Filling Your Time Well

As we partner with God in His work of renewing our hearts, we learn to stop giving in to our unhealthy cravings and instead start giving our time and attention to what our souls crave and need: Jesus. It's about shifting our focus from *How can I get more of this worldly thing?* to *How can I steward my time well for God?*

It's a little like how I learned to find a healthier approach to food. One of the greatest tips I learned along the way was upping my fiber and protein intake. Fiber is known to keep you regular (if you know what I'm saying), but it's also more filling than other nutrients, as is protein. These power-packed nutrients fill and satisfy your hunger and provide you with more energy to go about your day and maintain a healthy lifestyle.

Now, I'm not saying that God is fiber. I'm saying we crave satisfaction and fullness and yet we often go to short-lived solutions. We rely on fast food as our main source of nutrition. It may very well be delicious (hello, Chick-fil-A, I love you), but it does not give us true sustenance. When we feast instead on the Bread of Life, let Him be our primary source of satisfaction, and seek Him first, we're given the spiritual energy, strength, and fulfillment to handle all that life brings.

One of the most loving things God does is keep us from finding true joy, peace, and satisfaction in anything less than Him. We may find temporary hits of what we think are joy, peace, and satisfaction in the things outside of Him, but they are exactly that—temporary. Your heavenly Father is jealous for you, and you can count on His commitment, a commitment to not let us settle for anything less than Him in first place, because that's where a faithful life starts.

Reflection Questions

1. What temporary sources of fulfillment do you notice yourself craving and running to for satisfaction?
2. How can you start small today? What are some small steps you can take or small sacrifices you can make to retrain yourself to crave the Word more than the world?
3. Are there any things in your life that you need to submit to God? Pray and ask that He would give you the strength to trust Him fully in order to hand those things over.

FOUR

Remember Who You Are

Jesus came to announce to us that an identity based on success, popularity, and power is a false identity—an illusion! Loudly and clearly he says: "You are not what the world makes you; but you are children of God."

HENRI NOUWEN

I was barely five years old when I had my first run-in with comparison. Long before I had a smart phone, and long before the hype of influencers and affiliate links. It happened in my preschool ballet class, surrounded by a handful of other hopeful ballerinas. There was one girl in particular who stood out; let's call her Sissy. Sissy was one of my ballet teacher's favorite pupils, because she was flexible, athletic, and serious. Now, I would describe four-year-old Tara as athletic and serious but not so flexible. I could barely get my knees down in a butterfly stretch, let alone lie on my tummy, bend backward, and touch my toes to my head like Sissy could. While my peers and I hovered two feet above the ground in our pathetic splits, she plopped down without breaking a sweat.

Every day after class I sat down on my carpeted bedroom floor to stretch for at least thirty minutes. All because I wanted to be as flexible as Sissy. I wanted to be as praised and favored as Sissy was. It didn't matter how excellent of a little ballerina I was on my own, how much I was progressing and how quickly I caught on, or even how much better I was at the 6/8 allegro floor work than the rest of my class. It all came down to Sissy. I didn't just want to be *like* her. I wanted to *be* her, because she had the ballet life I wanted. From where I was standing, she had it all.

While I eventually conquered my battle of comparison

Overbooked and Overwhelmed

to Sissy, I moved on to the next battle. This time it was Erica from sixth grade. She had the best makeup, best clothes, and the most attention from the boys. Middle school Tara was as tomboy as you could imagine. While Erica and the other girls rocked gently and femininely on the swings and giggled about which boys they were crushing on, I was out playing football, soccer, basketball, and King of the Hill with the boys. Yet the moment I started comparing myself to Erica, I began wondering whether something was wrong with me. I wondered whether I should be doing things her way. So I started to dress differently. I donned poufs and flower headbands. I experimented with bright lipstick. Deep down inside, I hated it. But I wanted to be Erica. The more I looked to Erica as my standard, the more preoccupied and obsessed I became. And the less I focused on who God had created me to be.

Fast-forward ten years to my early twenties. Sissy and Erica had been out of my life for a long time, but—you guessed it—comparison was still alive and well. And it waltzed back into my life through the doorway of social media. Picture this: I was newly married and newly pregnant. I had zero clue what I was doing and was still reeling from the shocking positive pregnancy test. One of my first instincts was to take to social media to follow all the pregnant and mommy bloggers to give me direction.

Before I knew it, my Amazon cart was full of items these experienced moms raved were must-haves. Clothes, outfits, belly bands. And wouldn't you know it, I even started dressing like those influencers. I mapped out my son's nursery to look like their babies' nurseries. I spent a ridiculous amount of money, because I didn't just want my life to look like theirs, I wanted my life to *be* theirs. After receiving all my Amazon orders and dressing differently, I was surprised when I didn't feel any different. In fact, I felt worse.

I had held up my life in comparison to so many other people's lives for so long that I spiraled into self-loathing, envy, and jealousy. The moment when I realized just how far down comparison's path I had willingly walked was unsettling, to say the least. It was as if I had just snapped out of the most disorienting brain fog and was suddenly awake.

There's nothing wrong with finding inspiration from your favorite Instagram account or Pinterest feed. My feeds are full of the most inspiring dinner recipes, sourdough techniques, outfit inspirations, and biblical encouragement. They bring me so much joy. (I've lost track of how many times social media has saved my butt when I had no idea what to cook for dinner or when I was confused about sourdough crumb density.) There's beauty in gleaning insight from those who are in a similar season to ours or from one who has gone before. It's rather right and holy. But innocent inspiration is one thing; catastrophic comparison is another.

Psychology Today defines social comparison theory as "the idea that individuals determine their own social and personal worth based on how they stack up against others."[1] But you and I know that comparison isn't new. It's been around since the fall, and it's only amplified now with such

Overbooked and Overwhelmed

unfettered access to each other's lives online—filtered and unfiltered.

As a popular saying goes, "Comparison is the thief of joy." I would probably add to those wise words that comparison isn't just the thief of joy; comparison shifts our focus off who we are in the light of who God is and warps our ability to thrive in the life He has given us. It makes us forget our identities and, consequently, our purpose.

A few years ago, my parents asked me to be a guest speaker for the middle school youth group they lead. I thought back to the struggles I had dealt with at that age. The first thing that came to mind was identity—struggling to know who I was or, rather, Whose I was. Although there's something to be said about how tender we are as children when it comes to insecurity and identity, children are not the only ones who struggle to know who they are. And it's not just preteens and high schoolers who are searching for their identity and purpose. It's all of us.

So, at whatever age or stage of life, we must remember the beauty of our identities in Christ, recall the beautiful plan He gave us in the first place, and refocus on what matters so that we can live more awake to our purpose and less overwhelmed by the external. Because the truth is, knowing who God has purposed us to be is essential to remaining

> *Knowing who God has purposed us to be is essential to remaining firmly planted in a world that wants to tempt us to live for the temporary.*

firmly planted in a world that wants to tempt us to live for the temporary.

Who Are You Really?

I was nine years old when someone made fun of me for being Asian. One of my classmates was trying desperately to get a rise out of the crowds at lunchtime. He made fun of my almond eyes, asking, "Can you even see out of those? They're so tiny!" He mocked me with his best impression of an Asian language, shouting, "Ching, chang, chong! Tara knows what I'm saying!" I put on a brave face and nervously laughed with the ones who were laughing at me. I didn't want them to see that I was actually breaking inside.

I was raised by the most incredible parents; they never made my brother or me feel less than or unloved just because we didn't share the same DNA. My mom has blue eyes and curly blond hair. My dad has dark hair and a very German look about him. One glance and you would know my brother and I are not their biological children. But blood didn't matter to my parents. We weren't their second choice. We were always chosen by them. We were always theirs, and they were ours. But that little punk at the school lunch table threw me for a loop and made me wonder whether what his words suggested were true. In a sea of children who all looked the same—light skin, sun-drenched hair, and pale eyes—there I was, standing out as different. I wondered, *Am I worthy? Does my skin color actually make me less lovable and less important than kids with white skin?*

As I grew older I grew out of my insecurities about my skin color. But the seed of doubt about my identity lingered.

I didn't think I was placing my identity in work—my productivity, achievement, and efficiency—but my need to prove myself through how much I worked and overworked proved otherwise.

I didn't think my identity was in how much money I made or didn't make—until I saw myself riddled with stress and fatigue over chasing a number to make sure I wasn't a failure.

I didn't think my identity was in my physical health or fitness—until I started to question my value when a fibromyalgia flare-up caused me to lie in bed all week and not get anything done.

I didn't think my identity was in my relational or familial status—until in certain seasons I tried to make my role as a wife and mother seem put-together as proof that I was worthy.

I didn't think my identity was in my Instagram follower count, podcast downloads, or book sales—until I became a little more obsessed with algorithmic reach and demographics than with the kingdom of God.

What do all those misplaced identities have in common? I was looking to anything and everything except Christ to tell me who I was and give me something worth living for.

I was distracted by looking to other things for what I could find only in the finished work of the cross.

Our souls awaken to each new day searching for direction. For a plan. For a reason. For fulfillment. But what happens at the beginning of each new day? Life happens. Overwhelm happens. Work stress happens. School and future-planning anxiety happens. The intensity of mothering young children happens. The allure of social media comes knocking. All these things steal our soul's gaze, a gaze that is really only looking for God, the One who made us.

Social media cannot return the knowing and loving gaze—the affection, the devotion, and the security—that we crave. Money cannot return the knowing and loving gaze that we crave. Crushing it at work cannot return the knowing and loving gaze that we crave. We might not be able to put a finger on it, but what our souls are really looking for is God. And the good news is that He has looked upon us first.

This is the truth that empowers us to get out of bed in the morning and face both the highs and the lows. This is the truth that empowers us to cope with both success and missteps without losing our minds. This is the truth that empowers us to steward things like social media, entertainment, food, relationships, responsibilities, and all the distractions of life with grace and wisdom. Because, as we've been saying this whole time, it's not the distractions or our overbooked schedules themselves that are killing our souls; it's the power we allow them to have over our lives.

Overbooked and Overwhelmed

You Are

A mind distracted by the world is far more susceptible to carelessly forget the truth our souls desperately need. So, as any good friend would, I'm here to remind us of a truth that will never change or depart from us, no matter how careless we become. Let this tether you back to the heart of the Father: "You are a chosen race, a royal priesthood, a holy nation, a people for his own possession, that you may proclaim the excellencies of him who called you out of darkness into his marvelous light. Once you were not a people, but now you are God's people; once you had not received mercy, but now you have received mercy" (1 Peter 2:9–10).

Wow. Read that again. Let it sink in.

If you are in Christ, you have been *chosen*. You were not overlooked; rather, God looked on you with such love that it compelled Him to make you His own. And here's the cool domino effect. Your identity as a chosen child of God gives you a new calling. It commissions you with the authority of Christ to go and tell the world through your own little world—your own city, your own home, your own influence. God can and will use your work, schooling, ministry, home, relationship status, money, and even social media usage as avenues to work out His glorious purpose in your life. But don't forget: You were chosen to be devoted to God, not to those things. They are lousy obstacles of your heart's truest affection, which is meant to be Him.

You are also part of a *royal priesthood*. Your identity as a member of the royal priesthood means you have a new kind of access to God. You don't have to jump through hoops or ask a human priest to go to Him on your behalf. You can do that every single day. At your kitchen sink. In your cubicle. While you rock your baby to sleep. And you are royal. This means you have the status of a prince or princess. Magnificent. Noble. You are a child of the Most High. And in eternity's future, you can look forward to reigning with Him in glory because of what He accomplished on the cross.

On top of all that, you are part of *a holy nation*. To be holy means to be set apart, the opposite of distracted by the world. To be distinctly God's, faithful to Him. Jesus has made you—yes, *you*—holy. Say what? Anyone else feel a little less than holy on a daily basis? Anyone else struggle to not feel overwhelmed by your to-do list and your everyday tasks? Same. But here's the thing about holiness: It's an inherited part of our identity.

Before Jesus, we were tainted by the rule of sin. But after accepting Jesus, we are washed by His cleansing blood and repurposed for an eternity that is greater than the temporary. While holy is our reality, the world is loud and the temptations are strong. This means we must fight to remain set apart and unmoved by whatever wants to push us away from Christ. This means our job is to obey, yield, and follow the Spirit inside us who is cheering us on toward holiness.

I love the next part of 1 Peter 2. Peter calls us *a people for God's own possession*. Some other versions say, "His special people." Let's be honest: No one wants to be possessed or owned by anyone else. We've made much progress in this world where it is deplorable to own or be owned by other people. But in God's upside-down kingdom, possession is different. Here's what I mean. To possess something means to have, carry, take hold of. This possession is not a violent overtaking but a loving security and a special blessing.

What a wildly wonderful promise for us. What a sweet gift for a world longing to be known, seen, and heard. God has taken hold of us in the most loving embrace, and He has no intentions of letting go. But His embrace doesn't end there. His embrace empowers us to be vessels that are worthy of carrying the Holy Spirit. When we grasp the reality that we are held and secure in Christ, there is no distraction, temptation, or overwhelming circumstance that can shake us. That truth enables us to walk with a fixed and unhindered gaze, because nothing is strong enough to overwhelm the love of Christ in us.

And the last part: "That you may proclaim the excellencies of him who called you out of darkness into his marvelous light." This is what I want you to hold on to when the enemy, life's distractions, and overwhelming circumstances darken your vision and make you forget who you are. Satan operates in the dark and loves to coax us into the darkness with him, because it's in that very same darkness that we cannot see clearly. But hold fast to this truth: Just because life is dark does not mean the Light of the World is not there. It does not mean He is any less powerful or any less superior than whatever you're facing. You were called into His marvelous light. The darkness can feel overwhelming, yes. The darkness can be disorienting, yes. But you have been brought into the light, and in that light you can walk with deep assurance. When you are overwhelmed by the distractions around you, look to the Light. He will give you the clarity and confidence to see who He's made you to be and what you must lay down in order to pick up His purposes.

Don't Waste Your Life

A month after I graduated from high school, my family threw me a graduation party in our backyard. It was a hot July afternoon with my dad's famous barbecue meat, an iced-coffee bar, and all my favorite people. As much as I treasured that day, I was itching for the moment when I could rip into my pile of cards and presents. (Can you blame me? I was a soon-to-be college student and needed money for stuff like furniture, clothes, food, and tuition.) When that moment finally came, I tore through the pile lickety-split. One of the last gifts I opened was from a sweet couple I had gone to church with my whole life. Their card was taped to a book, John Piper's *Don't Waste Your Life*. I chuckled and thought to myself, *What an odd present*. I didn't think I needed a book to tell me not to waste my life.

I resisted opening this book for a while, so it just sat in my room unopened. Until one day when my curiosity got the best of me. The title gnawed at me, drawing out a fear I had deep inside: *What if I do waste my life?* I was at a pivotal transition point, going from living at home with my parents to moving out on my own and starting college, which would eventually launch me into my career. I flipped to the first page and began. My nonchalant reading quickly turned into intent study. I didn't just read the book; I filled an entire journal of notes to go along with what I was reading.

Years later, I found that journal for the first time since the summer of 2017. It was in a storage box with a ton of random memorabilia from high school. Fondly, I flipped through it. My fingers brushed to the last page, and my eyes landed on the very last sentence I had written.

Will this matter for eternity?

This is a question I had forgotten, a question I had stopped asking myself as the distractions stole my focus and attention from God. I had started looking to the world and those around me to define who I was, looking to my achievements, my comfort, and my circumstances instead of to Christ. I had lost sight of the long term, the reason that I existed, and the person that I existed to glorify.

When we are not secure in our identity in Christ, everything else suffers.

When we forget that we are chosen, we'll look to the world to affirm us through what we achieve.

When we forget that we were put here on earth to be stewards and managers of God's good gifts, we'll start living for the temporary.

When we forget that God calls us holy, we'll be tempted

to go with culture and allow little loves to become greater than our first love.

In one of my favorite quotes from *Don't Waste Your Life*, John Piper talks about how easily we forget who God has called us to be:

> I am wired by nature to love the same toys that the world loves. I start to fit in. I start to love what others love. I start to call earth "home." Before you know it, I am calling luxuries "needs" and using my money just the way unbelievers do. I begin to forget the war. I don't think much about people perishing. Missions and unreached peoples drop out of my mind. I stop dreaming about the triumphs of grace. I sink into a secular mind-set that looks first to what man can do, not what God can do. It is a terrible sickness. And I thank God for those who have forced me again and again toward a wartime mind-set.[2]

I've always had a sharp memory. The barista I met at a random coffee shop last week? I remember her name. The new checker at the grocery store? I remember his name. The sweet couple and their five kids who attended church for the first time last Sunday? I remember their names. But then I wonder, *Why is it that I can remember all these names, but I am so forgetful of what God says about who I am?*

The bottom line is, we're forgetful people. Not because we're not smart or intelligent but because the more our brains take on, and the more responsibilities and stressors there are

Overbooked and Overwhelmed

on us, the easier it is to be forgetful and lose space for what matters most. Our brains become a mess of information overload, and it leaves little room or energy for much else. Before writing this chapter I lost my AirPods. Know where I found them? In my front pocket. That's why we need to train.

We need Ebenezer stones of identity in our lives. In the Old Testament, God's people set up Ebenezers, stone altars or physical places that commemorated God's work. They were tangible ways to remember what He had done for His people. God knew that His people needed an obvious, in-their-face reminder of His goodness, faithfulness, and truth. A place to return to for hope when life got hard, suffering came, their enemies closed in, or they were tempted to look to idols and distractions to satisfy. We need Ebenezer stones in our lives, too, to remind us of who God is, what He's done, and who we are in His light.

"Bind my wandering heart to thee," Robert Robinson wrote in 1758.[3] What can we do today to bind our hearts to God's truth—who He is and who He has made us to be? What if it is as simple as journaling and cataloging truths from Scripture to refer to every morning or every night? As simple as memorizing 1 Peter 2:9–10 or any other powerful verse on identity to tuck in our minds for moments of weakness? As simple as putting sticky notes of God's attributes on our bathroom mirrors? As simple as making our phone wallpaper a passage of Scripture? As simple as taking a social media fast and replacing our Instagram app with an audio Bible to carry us through our day?

Remember Who You Are

May we be proactive about setting up those Ebenezer stones now, so that when we get overwhelmed by life (which we will), when life attempts to knock us down (which it will), or when we feel the tug to ignore Jesus and not prioritize our relationship with Him (which we all know can happen), we can tether ourselves back to the reality that He is better. Say this with me: *He is where my worth comes from. He is where my fulfillment rests. I know the enemy wants to distract me from God by tempting me to waste my time on trivial things. But here I raise my Ebenezer.*

I don't want to reach the end of my life and realize that I wasted it. I don't want to reach the end of my life and realize that I did not live aware of eternity or that my time on earth is precious. So here's my last warning and encouragement for you: Wasting your life doesn't happen because you didn't make enough money. It doesn't happen because of not breaking ceilings, not reaching a million followers on TikTok, or failing your chemistry class. A wasted life happens when we forget who God is—His goodness, His truth, and His commission—and what He made us for.

Your identity will rise and fall when you put it in temporary things and distractions. But when you place your identity in Christ, you will stand tall. In that standing tall, in that firm foundation, you can run your race with clarity and confidence with a fixed, unhindered gaze, devoted to a call and to a Savior who will never let you down.

A wasted life happens when we forget who God is—His goodness, His truth, and His commission—and what He made us for.

Remember Who You Are

Reflection Questions

1. List a few names or identities that God has given you (example: loved, precious, purposed). Make a physical or mental list so that you are prepared when the overwhelming circumstances of life try to take your eyes off Him.
2. Are there people, places, or things you have been placing your identity in other than Jesus? If so, acknowledge them and bring them to light. Who or what are they?
3. What Ebenezer stones of your identity in Christ and His love for you can you practically implement in your everyday life?

FIVE

Choose the Better Portion

*If we want our lives to work, the
Jesus-first life is the way.*

LISA WHITTLE

Imagine you have a glass jar on your countertop, along with some golf balls, sand, and gravel. The jar represents your life. The golf balls represent the most important things in your life: God, your relationship with Him, and the ways you spend time with Him—journaling, worshiping, praying, for example. The sand and gravel represent all the other things: work, school, relationships, ministry, exercise, social media, everything else that fills your time. If you put the golf balls in first, then the sand and gravel pieces fill in around them. But if you fill your jar with the sand and gravel first, then there's hardly any room left for the golf balls. They come tumbling out of the jar because they were added last. My literary agent, or "book mom" as I affectionately call her, told me this illustration a few years ago and I will never forget it. It shows that order matters. How you prioritize matters.

Our relationship with God was never intended to be the golf ball we toss in last. Our relationship with God is meant to be the foundation of our existence.

We see this dichotomy played out in a story woven into God's narrative about two women—one who filled her days with busyness first and the other who saw the beauty and blessing of putting her Savior first. Who are these two women? I bet you can guess. It's Mary and Martha.

Overbooked and Overwhelmed

I don't know about you, but I've heard many a pastor or influencer proclaim, "Be a Mary, not a Martha!" While I get the sentiment behind that statement, can we push back on that Martha-hating narrative just a little? Where exactly was Martha coming from with her side of the story? Let's start with how the Bible tells it:

> As Jesus and the disciples continued on their way to Jerusalem, they came to a certain village where a woman named Martha welcomed him into her home. Her sister, Mary, sat at the Lord's feet, listening to what he taught. But Martha was distracted by the big dinner she was preparing. She came to Jesus and said, "Lord, doesn't it seem unfair to you that my sister just sits here while I do all the work? Tell her to come and help me."
>
> But the Lord said to her, "My dear Martha, you are worried and upset over all these details! There is only one thing worth being concerned about. Mary has discovered it, and it will not be taken away from her." (Luke 10:38–42 NLT)

Slip on Martha's shoes with me, won't you? Jesus, the Messiah, is coming to eat at your home. Talk about the most important event on your calendar. You'll want the house to be spotless, the ambiance relaxing, and your meal to leave mouths watering for more. It's natural to feel distracted, frenzied, and overstimulated by the responsibility of hosting the King of kings in your home. Now add the societal and cultural norms to that internalized pressure. In Near Eastern tradition, hosting was held in high esteem and to an even higher standard than what we're used to today. If you, as the host, did anything to dishonor or disgrace your guests, dishonor and disgrace would be piled higher on you.

It's completely fair and justified that you would be "distracted by much serving" with the number of trips you must take out to the well to satisfy your guests' thirst. Of course, you would be "worried over all these details," such as whether the leaven in your bread had risen enough or how to arrange your furniture to accommodate everyone. No one would fault you for being overwhelmed. This is an important task, and it is surely pulling your attention in a million different directions.

Now slip your own shoes back on. I don't know about you, but I felt strangely at home in Martha's shoes. I melted almost seamlessly into that narrative. We're told in Luke 10 that she was distracted by the big dinner she was preparing. Other versions say "much serving." The verbiage here is purposeful. She wasn't preoccupied by something little or trivial but by many responsibilities, and good and righteous responsibilities at that. The author is not diminishing the validity of Martha's tasks. Serving itself and her desire to be an admirable host for Jesus were not the problems. Anxiety and worry were the problems.

Worry about not getting things done.
Anxiety over not doing the right things.
Worry about not looking put-together.
Anxiety over not measuring up.

Her priorities skewed her well-intended service. She was filling her jar with anxiety and worry first. Where was Jesus—where were the golf balls—to go?

I can just picture Martha slaving at the counter and spotting her sister, Mary, out of the corner of her eye, sitting at Jesus' feet. Bristling to herself, Martha has finally had it. She blurts out, "Lord, I'm doing all the work here. Can't You see me?"

Ding, ding. That's it. That's the point here. Martha wants to be seen, known, and loved. She is distracted by fear, not devoted in love. Jesus responds with a gentle ease, "My dear Martha, you are worried and upset over all these details!" The Messiah's words reveal Martha's true motivation for her distraction. Marshall Segal described it this way for Desiring God: "Martha was distracted from Jesus because her mind was drowning in the cares of this world. And because she would not stop and listen to Jesus, she was forfeiting the calm she so desperately needed."[1]

Doing without devotion. I like to think that what drove Martha to worry was thinking about how her house looked, how her guests felt, or how impressed Jesus was by her hosting abilities. I like to think that she was anxiously hoping this night would reflect well on her. But when doing without devotion, doing without the right heart, or doing with a mindset of distraction is our motivator, we will never be able to truly rest in Jesus. We will never be able to prioritize His presence.

"One thing is necessary," Jesus said. "Mary has chosen the good portion, which will not be taken away from her"

(v. 42). Jesus didn't want the leftovers of Martha's heart. He wanted her, all of her. He wanted to show her that when she surrendered all to Him, His power and ability would overflow into every other aspect of her life.

Then the focus of the story shifts to the second sister, Mary. She would not fare well in our modern-day culture. A culture that praises multitasking, overcommitting, overstimulation, and girl-bossing would throw her out the door if they saw that she just sat at the feet of Jesus. But much like Jesus' kingdom, Mary did the upside-down thing. She was the holy anomaly. She did not overbook herself in that moment. She decided that the to-do lists and distractions, all the things vying for her attention, were not needed in the moment. Not that they weren't important at all, but that they weren't the most important in comparison to filling her cup first with Jesus.

Doing things was not the prerequisite; there were no boxes needing to be checked off before she sat with Jesus. Her posture was humble. She was open, exposed, and receptive. She cared more about what He said than what others thought about her or her home. She cared more about listening to Jesus than listening to the world.

Martin Luther has been widely quoted as once saying, "I have so much to do that I shall spend the first three hours in prayer." Although praying for three hours sounds wonderful and downright impressive, it also sounds pretty unrealistic when you and I have jobs, families, and responsibilities. But the point Luther was emphasizing is deeper than that. When our calendars are overwhelming, when life is full, and when we're distracted by much, the answer isn't to keep doing. (Although I'll be the first to admit that is my tendency.) The answer isn't to pick up the pace or heap more distractions onto our plates, although that is sometimes the message culture sends. The answer is to sit at the feet of Jesus, listen, and put Him first. Maybe you don't have three hours to put before your laundry list of tasks. The idea is just that you put Jesus first.

What does it mean to put Jesus first, you ask? It's the idea of esteeming Jesus as higher and more valuable than anyone or anything this world has to offer. And to do that we have to learn how to slow down. The most urgent, the most important thing in life is really Jesus Himself. And so we don't miss Him in the hustle and bustle, we must slow and steady our souls. We must keep up with Him first, rather than feel the need to keep up with the world. And as we prioritize walking with Jesus, we're freed up to steward the responsibilities and distractions in a healthy and holy way, just as Mary did.

Here are a few principles to keep in mind as we're learning to walk in Mary's footsteps.

DISTRACTION IS NOT A DISORDERED SCHEDULE. IT'S A DISORDERED HEART IN NEED OF TRANSFORMATION. The pressures, anxieties, and distractions of hosting revealed that Martha's heart was cluttered, and that influenced how she engaged Jesus in her home. Martha's external circumstances only amplified her disordered heart.

DISTRACTION CAN AFFECT OUR SPIRITUAL DEVOTION. If we're not careful, it's far too easy to forget that our thoughts and actions affect our spirit. Martha let her mental distraction, her worries, and her preoccupations affect the health of her spirit. All those things filled her jar and distracted her from tending to her soul first. When we choose to prioritize spiritual devotion, it enables us to handle the fullness, busyness, and temptations of this world.

DEVOTION IS CHOOSING THE BEST PORTION. DISTRACTION WILL ALWAYS BE CHOOSING THE LESSER. Jesus loved Martha so much that He called her in gentleness and holiness to transform her thinking, which would transform her heart, and then transform the way she lived. To Martha, her sister's priorities may have seemed out of order, but Mary's heart was in the right place. Jesus said it best. Mary chose the better portion, and that was a blessing no one could take away from her. Not even her frustrated sister. Devotion is the best choice, and distraction is the lesser. How often do we believe the lie that the best portion is found in lesser places?

Is Jesus Really Enough?

I was raised by God-fearing parents who genuinely loved the Lord. I attended church every Sunday and sat under sound biblical teaching. I was surrounded by community and family members who spoke the truth to me on a regular basis. And yet, for a long season of my life, I was the girl who preached "Jesus is enough for me, and Jesus is enough for you!" but simultaneously lived to the contrary. I reshared posts on Instagram and wrote captions that proclaimed the satisfaction found in Jesus alone but hypocritically lived for other things to fill me up.

You see, that's the thing about distraction. It's not just a momentary lapse in our attention span. I wish it were as harmless as that. What it actually does is affect our souls over time. Distraction is a forgetfulness of just how good, better, and enough Jesus is in comparison to everything else. If we allow our souls to become so rushed, so overwhelmed, and so overworked, our lives may just shift our focus away from the satisfaction found in Christ. It's subtle and seductive, beginning with whispers that we are lacking and that we need something else to fill us, our calendars, and our attention spans. Other things start to look much better and much more appealing than Christ. Then, all of a sudden, He's not first anymore.

If you read my first book, *Surrender Your Story*, you know how my husband and I met and the obsession I had with getting engaged. We started dating when we were seventeen. Dating during high school was a lot of fun and not dissimilar to how romantic comedies portray it. We went to football games, flirted across the room during class, hung out after school, and went on adventurous dates. But after we graduated, something happened. I started to become more and more impatient and obsessed with getting an engagement ring. And I'm not talking a cute kind of obsessed. It was full-on manic.

Although marriage is a good desire and a gift from God,

it became an enslaving craving and a detrimental distraction. In retrospect, I see that it was a snare that the enemy used to take my eyes off what mattered most: Jesus. My impatience over becoming a Mrs. consumed my thoughts, instead of whatever is true, noble, right, pure, lovely, admirable, excellent, or praiseworthy (Philippians 4:8 NIV). Nearly every day, I complained and whined that I wasn't engaged, and I became bitterly green when I saw other people post their engagement rings on Instagram. I was so focused on where I wanted to be that I couldn't enjoy where I was.

You know that saying about anger? "All I could see was red"? Well, you could say that about me, except all I could see was white. White wedding dresses. I lived through that lens of longing with the belief that when I got what I wanted, *then* I would feel satisfied. *Then* Jesus would be enough. Life was formulaic.

Jesus + marriage = satisfaction
Jesus + thing that I wanted = wholeness
Jesus + achievement = success

I was getting it all wrong. I felt spiritually apathetic and distant from God. And not because of Michael but because of what I prioritized—an idolization of marriage first and the Giver of marriage second. The truth was, Jesus didn't need any additions to be enough for me. But my vision was clouded by what I wanted. I was under the influence, you might say.

Overbooked and Overwhelmed

The phrase "under the influence" is primarily used to describe someone intoxicated by alcohol. While I can say that I have never been intoxicated by alcohol, I *have* been under the influence of many other things: social media, influencers, family, friends, finances, you name it. Our society is wildly consumeristic. We think the more we buy, the more we have, the happier we will be. Pick yourself up by the bootstraps, perfect this life hack, do your skin-care routine, buy this gadget, build an empire, gain social media followers, accumulate wealth, retire early, get enough sleep, and then you'll be enough. Then you'll have enough. This is the gospel of culture, not the gospel of Christ.

The real gospel, the real good news, is that Jesus is the Living Water (John 7:38). Jesus is the Bread of Life (John 6:35). Jesus is the Rock on which we stand (1 Corinthians 10:4). Jesus is the True Vine (John 15:1). What do all those names have in common? The fact that Jesus is enough. He is our source. He is our salvation. He is sufficient. He is the answer. He is abundantly, completely, and truly everything we need. About whom or what else can we say the same?

Now, I hear you. Let's not be naive. Every single day, without fail, you and I have essential needs like food, water, shelter, and clothing. I'm not lobbying for us to all stop eating or wearing clothes. God created our bodies to need those things, as well as community and connection, to name a few more. But the point is this: No one else saves and satisfies our souls like Jesus can.

Too many of us are walking around with a scarcity

mindset. Too many of us are living like we are lacking, so we keep on overbooking our schedules and our souls, searching for something to fill the void. Maybe you really do believe that Jesus is enough for you and that He deserves first place in your life. You've read it in the Bible, and you've heard it in Sunday school, but the very real busyness and heaviness of life has caused a lapse in memory. The very real appeal of social media and entertainment is alluring. I get it. That's why, my dear friend, we need a spiritual reset. Each day, we need a reminder of just how enough Jesus is:

> Jesus is enough to save us from death and hell. (Acts 4:12)
> Jesus is enough to provide for our every need. (Matthew 6:25–34; Psalm 23)
> Jesus is enough to equip and strengthen us. (Philippians 2:13; Ephesians 2:10)
> Jesus is enough to satisfy our deepest longings. (Psalm 107:9)
> Jesus is enough to bless us and fulfill us. (Ephesians 1:3)

Whenever I'm tempted to place something above Jesus, I ask myself this question: *Is Jesus' death, burial, and resurrection enough for me? If all I had was my salvation, would that be enough?* It's a sobering thought, no? If you've put your faith in Jesus Christ, your identity in Him is the best thing about you. You have invited Him to be the Lord of your life.

So let me ask you this: What's in your jar? Think about

the depth and breadth of your life. If this feels like a hard question to answer, think about your daily activities, your responsibilities, your vocation, your education, your people, and your relationship with God. Think about who and what you give your time to. The first step in finding your enoughness in Christ is asking yourself what other things are in competition.

You Have a Choice

Some experts claim that distraction is a good thing. Research scholar Ian Fiebelkorn asserts that "the brain can't process everything in the environment. . . . It's developed those filtering processes that allow it to focus on some information at the expense of other information."[2] To an extent, I agree. There's just no way to focus solely on God twenty-four hours a day, seven days a week, 365 days a year, without anything else stealing our attention. Scientific research shows that our brains were not made to operate that way, and they've also been affected as time and technology have trudged on, with our attention spans weakening, our tension headaches heightening, and our anxiety and stress elevating. But the article goes on to say that we "might as well stop trying" to focus and give in to our "evolutionary" instincts. That's where I disagree.

I won't sit here and pretend that the scientific studies and physiological evidence aren't real. But it's the stubborn, strong-willed side of me speaking when I say that we're not going to stop trying. We're not going to settle, are we, friend? God's Word tells us that no matter how many distractions, temptations, and overwhelming situations we have in a day, it is possible to keep Him first as our steady foundation and our heart's affection. As disciples of Jesus, we do not have to bend or break at the first sight of resistance. In fact, resistance is exactly what fortifies physical and spiritual muscles.

Our brains may be overwhelmed by the pace of life, but our hearts don't have to be. Our lives may be overbooked and frantic, but our hearts don't have to be. In Christ we have the power and ability to remain steady and focused on Him, even when the wind and the waves are rocking our boats. When we dwell on the vertical—Jesus who reigns over us— we can handle the horizontal distractions of life. Let your vertical relationship with Jesus influence how you interact with the world, your busy schedule, and all the things vying for your time and attention.

Maybe you're tracking with me thus far but are wondering how you're supposed to let Jesus influence your schedule when, with each new day, you're presented with another set of distractions and other important responsibilities to check off your to-do list. Spending more time with Jesus may sound doable in the moment, but how can you make it a sustainable lifestyle when the overwhelm, busyness, and interruptions of tomorrow are looming? I have three words for you: Start again tomorrow.

My dad has always told people that he is a rather simple

follower of Jesus. He has never had any formal, academic training in the Bible, but anyone who knows him or has been his student in Sunday school knows that he knows God and His Word because he walks with Him daily. I remember going to him for advice when I was a young child whenever following Jesus felt complicated and hard to stay committed to. I'll never forget what he told me once: "You know, Tara, I just wake up every morning and pray this prayer. To some it may feel simple, but to me it's powerful. 'Father, I love You and I want to follow You today. Help me to do just that, amen.'"

That has been my daily prayer for almost a decade. (Thanks, Dad.) The reality is, each day we are faced with hundreds, if not thousands, of choices. Choices about schooling, work, parenthood, ministry, homemaking, relationships, the future, what you're going to make for dinner, how many loads of laundry you're going to try to squeeze in, you name it. But what my dad was illustrating was that putting Jesus first is a daily choice. It's starting again tomorrow and the next day and the next day, until we are fully satisfied in eternity with Jesus. It's letting the overwhelm and intensity of the day push you further into the arms of Jesus. But if this all sounds exhausting to you, can I remind you that there's so much grace wrapped up in taking it one day at a time?

There's grace for you today, and there's grace for you tomorrow. God's grace pours out into our lives daily, allowing us to handle what's in front of us. It's from the kindness and mercy of our Father's heart that we are able to depend on Him to face the unique situations of each day. You don't have to take life head-on, all at once. How exhausting would that be? If you have put your faith in Jesus Christ, you have His sufficiency coursing through your veins. You have His power and His grace and His mercy to start again today. To start again tomorrow. To make a choice that leads to life. And the truth is, when we choose Jesus first, life is much more doable.

I'm not saying this will be perfect—heck, I can name about twenty things that have already tempted me away from God today and it's not even noon! But when we get back to devoting our hearts to Jesus first, then we're given the ability to handle the busy schedules, overwhelming responsibilities, and to-do lists with grace. I can't speak for Mary, but I would guess that the time she prioritized Jesus' presence over her hosting duties gave her a renewed strength and focus to steward the mundane and magical of this thing called life.

Choose the good portion, friend, and it will not be taken away from you. The blessing that comes into your life from putting Jesus first will never be taken away from you. Even when life is busy. Choose this day to turn your heart toward the Lord instead of your growing to-do list, and you will find the true peace, fulfillment, and satisfaction you've been longing for.

When we choose *Jesus first,* life is much more doable.

Choose the Better Portion

Reflection Questions

1. Who do you relate to more in this moment, Mary or Martha? Why?
2. What things might God be calling you to lay down, pause, or say no to in order to choose the better portion, as Mary did?
3. Ask yourself this question and answer honestly: *Is Jesus and His salvation really enough for me without any additions?* Read John 1:1–18 and remind yourself of the gospel and His sufficiency.

SIX

Prioritize His Presence

To experience Him should be to know beauty.
To hear from Him should be your soul's food.
To obey Him should be a sustaining joy.

FAITH EURY CHO

At one thirty in the morning, when I was forty weeks and three days pregnant, Michael and I rushed to the hospital, because I was convinced the time had come to have a baby after some intense labor pains at home. But after we waited in triage, the sweetest night nurse checked me and promptly sent me home with the disappointing news that I was only one centimeter dilated. Little did I know that just eight hours later, at my previously scheduled appointment, my doctor would tell me that I had dilated enough in that short time to have the baby. Talk about a whirlwind. Although my body had been warming up for the grand finale for months and we mentally knew our son was coming, nothing could have prepared us for what was next. Life would never be the same.

Everyone told us that the newborn days would feel like walking around in a fog—dazed, confused, and exhausted. After all, we were entering into a new normal that we had no prior context for. You would think that after Hunter started sleeping through the night, my milk supply regulated from engorged to normal, and we got our daily routine somewhat ironed out, the world would be right again. Wrong. While our circumstances settled, my brain did not.

Research says that a woman's brain changes after having a baby, that her gray-matter levels lower, on top of all the other hormonal shifts going on inside her body.[1] To give you a quick science lesson: Gray matter is a valuable part of the central nervous system and plays a critical role in processing information and supporting things such as memory, emotions, and decision-making.[2] To all the moms reading this: You're not crazy. There's scientific proof that how you're feeling—flustered, scattered, and absent-minded—is real and is because of the chemical changes your body is undergoing. But I wouldn't say this feeling of overwhelm and disconnect is common only to mothers. It's also something nurses, executives, ministry leaders, students, empty nesters, homesteaders, and others experience. Working, raising children, studying, illness, loss, and the stress of daily living can lead to feelings of overwhelm and subsequent disengagement—so much so that it becomes hard to focus on what matters most, to show up fully present in our relationship with Jesus.

What about you? Do you ever feel like you're not fully present in your life and relationship with God? Life—with all its responsibilities, to-dos, circumstances, surprises, and distractions—is happening so fast that it feels nearly impossible to keep up. However hard the challenge, however overwhelming life is, your core desire is to live unhindered by life's burdens and demands. You want to be a present wife, mother, student, leader, teacher, associate, worker (insert your role here), *but* you're constantly pulled in so many different directions. That leads us to a pivotal crossroads and a pivotal question: Is "present" really possible?

What would happen if we stopped waiting around for the perfect, serene circumstances and an empty calendar to prioritize the presence of God and, instead, met Him right where we were? Maybe what we really need to do is relearn what it means to dwell with Him and prioritize His presence. And when we do that, we will be better equipped to steward whatever life has to throw at us.

God Is at Home with You

If you go to church regularly, spend time in the Bible, or are involved in a small group, the idea of God's presence is not new to you. When we lose a loved one, people pray that God's presence would be with us. When we walk through a fiery trial or feel swallowed up by the depths of depression, they say, "God is with you." We sing songs about it in church, we whisper it in our prayers, and we say it to encourage others. My point is, we all know that God is with us, ever present and always near. But are we actually living like God is near to us and we are near to Him? Have we lost the meaning in the words "God is with us"?

In Bible times there were no townhouses, apartments, or condos. The places people lived were called "dwelling places," a fancy term for tents or mud houses. But God's presence surpassed physical walls. His plan was to dwell with His people. To stay with, remain with, and live with, no matter where they lived and no matter what their dwelling places looked like. God's plan all along was to provide a refuge, shelter, and habitation for His people that would weather the storms of life and give them the rest they were wandering around longing for. That dwelling place was Himself. There was never a plan B.

In the Old Testament Moses witnessed the presence of God through a burning bush, and there are countless other stories of God's presence manifested through miraculous signs and wonders. Eventually God set up camp and dwelled with His people primarily through the tabernacle, a place where only priests could go on behalf of the people. But in the New Testament God sent Jesus and His Spirit, who became a permanent home not bound by four walls or limited only to priests but completely accessible and available to anyone. The incredible news is that you and I live in the finished work of Jesus on the cross. We don't have to ask a priest to go into the sacred, roped-off presence of God for us—we can do that in our homes, in our cars, at our desks, and while we wash our dirty dishes. The Spirit is alive and well and available in every moment.

But can we get brutally honest for a second? How many of us have invited Jesus into our homes but are hardly ever there to spend time with Him? How many of us have allowed our house to become cluttered with distractions and forgotten that the King of kings lives not just *with* us but *in* us? How many of us give Jesus a brief, cursory glance during our days and never really stop to be present with Him?

When Hunter turned one month old, I realized that I hadn't opened my Bible and spent time in the Word since he was born. Thirty days I left my Bible untouched. The deceiver whispered shame over my soul, craftily convincing me that, because I had been away for so long, God would meet me with condemnation. The easier thing to do would have been to listen to the snake. To stay away, leave my Bible on the shelf, and keep God at arm's length. But the reality is that the farther we stray from God, the longer we stay away, and the more we give in to distraction, the harder it is to live all in for God.

But now's the time to step on the snake. Friend, if you have been giving everything and everyone else your time and attention, God will always welcome you back into His presence with loving arms when you turn back toward Him.

Romans 8 gives it to us straight: "Nothing can ever separate us from God's love. Neither death nor life, neither angels nor demons, neither our fears for today nor our worries about tomorrow—not even the powers of hell can separate us from God's love. No power in the sky above or in the earth below—indeed, nothing in all creation will ever be able to separate us from the love of God that is revealed in Christ Jesus our Lord" (vv. 38–39 NLT).

Nothing. Nothing can separate us from the love of Jesus. God has never left you, and He never will. His presence is always present. Just as the father did with his prodigal son, He welcomes us home time and time again (Luke 15:11–32).

I wonder whether it's easy to allow our relationship with God to flounder because we haven't completely grasped the reality that He is the most devoted to and in love with us. That is our starting place. When Christ is your home, you are always loved, always treasured, and always prioritized.

Overbooked and Overwhelmed

When you put Him first and when you regularly come into awareness of His presence in your life, you will see the weights, burdens, and overwhelm of life begin to lose their power over you. You will see that rhythmically prioritizing the presence of God gives you the tools to handle the stress and fullness of life, while putting distractions in their proper place.

Proximity Is Greater Than Productivity

Although I wasn't totally aware of it at the time, I got really good at living a double life. It was easy for me to show up every day and rattle off a list of my important tasks and responsibilities in ministry. The narrative I portrayed, on- and offline, to my friends and family was that my relationship with God was thriving when it was actually being overlooked.

I believed that my *productivity* for God automatically meant I was living in close *proximity* to Him—that the number of things I did in His name directly translated to how strong my relationship was with Him. Every day my calendar was jam-packed with things I had to do, share, post, and create. But I soon realized being productive for God had become a cheap counterfeit to experiencing the presence of God.

Getting away with God to sit in His presence for even

five minutes feels like pulling teeth for some of us. How can we "be still, and know that [He is] God" (Psalm 46:10) when there are a million other things to do? Everyone I know is asking that question. We sit down to read our Bibles and can barely get through one sentence before our minds are pulled to another thought, another worry, another task. We try to keep Jesus at the forefront of our thoughts during our daily routines, but sooner or later we're frustrated and fed up with how hard it is to connect with Jesus. We wonder how much easier it would be to be face-to-face with Jesus like Peter, James, and John were. It's just not the same.

> *Being productive for God is a cheap counterfeit to experiencing the presence of God*

It's true. It's not the same. It's better. Jesus said, "It is best for you that I go away, because if I don't, the Advocate won't come. If I do go away, then I will send him to you" (John 16:7 NLT). Limited to His human frame, Jesus couldn't be everywhere, always, all at once. Where His feet were was where He was. Jesus had to travel by foot or by donkey to get where He wanted to go—which usually took hours, if not days. But after He was killed, raised to life, and ascended to heaven, He introduced the Advocate, the Holy Spirit, to the entire world.

It's in your best interest that Jesus does not take up flesh and physically sit with you on your couch. Why? Because unlike Jesus in His human frame, the Holy Spirit is not limited to time or location. He can be everywhere for all people.

The Spirit makes it possible for me, for you, for those across the sea, and those down the street to always experience the power and the presence of God.

In The Seeking, You Are Seen

If the Spirit is with us at all times, how do we intentionally prioritize Him in our messy middle? In our weakness, our exhaustion, our overwhelming schedules, our distracted minds, and our important responsibilities?

May I give a suggestion? Seek God first. Contrary to what we believe, those three words are more than a cute Instagram blurb. They are more than a murmur on our lips. Seek God first. For followers of Christ, seeking God means setting our minds and hearts on Him. Practically, this is lived out through making Him our main motivation. By setting our minds on what He says over what anyone else says. By doing what He would want us to do over what culture would want us to do.

Imagine a car, maybe your car, rolling down a hill in neutral. It coasts without effort, without constraints, and without any intervention from the engine. Our minds have a similar function that, if we're not careful, we can easily slip into—neutral, merely coasting through life, not awake to God's truth that paves the way to living a meaningful life. When life gets hard, overwhelming, and overstimulating, one alluring option is to coast. Shrink back. Play it safe in our faith. Zone out. Keep our heads down. Although coasting may feel like a temporary, harmless reprieve from the intensity of life, coasting also causes us to drift. A car in neutral is at the mercy of its environment and gravity. There is no telling what kind of oncoming traffic the car could drift into. There is no telling how it could veer off course or affect the environment around it.

The abundant life Jesus spoke of in John 10:10 isn't a neutral-gear life. It's a life that graciously requires we show up, even when we're ragged and worn out, knowing full well that God is not ashamed of our exhaustion. He loves us at our best and our worst.

It's a conscious commitment to set our focus and attention on God. But setting our minds and hearts on God means we must be present. We must give our effort, even if it feels small, knowing that we don't have to produce kingdom results on our own, because the Spirit is the One who empowers us.

I've discovered that the more I allow overwhelm to consume me and the less I spend time in the presence of God, the more unsteady I feel in every aspect of life. But the more I spend time in His presence, digesting His truth, listening to what He has to say, and growing in His likeness, the more rooted and sure my life feels.

When I was growing up, the game hide-and-go-seek was a household favorite. My brother and I played it nearly every time we were with our childhood best friends. (The oldest of our group still suggests playing it to this day, and we're all in our mid- to late twenties. Never grow up, Matthew. We love that about you.) The older we got, the more inventive and intense the hiding spots became. One time my brother climbed nearly ten feet in the air to lie on top of our kitchen cabinets. That one took a while for us to figure out. Another time, I jammed myself into the very back of the upstairs linen closet and had my friend conceal me by putting the linens over me. And that's when I experienced claustrophobia for the first time. My point? The objective of hide-and-go-seek is to look for someone who is already there. In our minds that person is lost, but in all reality, they are very present. We just have to seek them out.

Same goes for God. He might seem lost when, in fact, He's very present. We just have to actively look for Him. You and I have to get around or through whatever is in our way, whatever is keeping us from experiencing His presence. My friend, this is what seeking God is! If life were an unobstructed, straightforward path, our task wouldn't be called seeking. The most meaningful relationships require work. Think about it: Jesus went to the cross for us, so now we are empowered to push through what's in the way to get more of Him.

Consider this your reminder to not accept defeat when things get in the way, because they will. Don't give up when life gets full, distractions are abundant, and God feels far off. Push through the noise and get around what's in the way. He is there. This is not to say that we should forsake the people, places, and things God has set in front of us. This just means that there should be a difference in our heart posture toward them. When our distractions and our responsibilities are first in our lives, their ways will determine our steps. When God is first in our lives, His Word and His ways will determine and guide our steps.

Prioritizing His Presence

I wonder whether we've made seeking God more complicated than it needs to be. Like a lot of things in Christian culture, I fear we've overcomplicated it by adding rules and regulations that Christ never put there. God does reveal Himself to us every day—in every moment, in the ordinary, the extraordinary, and also in the messy middle. So, as we're learning together how to prioritize His presence, let's consider these simple ways to regularly get face-to-face with Him.

SEEK GOD FIRST WITH YOUR TIME AND YOUR DECISIONS.

When was the last time you planned your life with God instead of planning God around your life? One simple way to seek God first is by consulting Him in how you plan your day. Find ways to glorify Him and set appointed times to be with Him instead of trying to just shove Him in as an afterthought.

You can do something similar with your decisions too.

When you're trying to decide whether to say yes or no to something, ask yourself, *Will this glorify God and draw me closer to Him?* If the answer is no, then you'll know it's only going to lead you away from Him and may not be what you want to do.

SEEK GOD FIRST BY READING THE WORD AND THROUGH PRAYER.

The Word of God is our compass, pointing us in the direction of deeper intimacy with Him. If we're consuming more of the world and letting its voice be louder than Christ's, then we're going to veer off course. So we need to regularly return to the compass of His Word and listen to His voice through prayer to help us stay on track.

SEEK GOD FIRST THROUGH CREATION AND CREATIVITY.

Don't discount the unconventional ways of seeking God. Maybe for you seeking God looks like praising Him and His good creation in your body while you work out. Maybe it's taking a drive or hiking and praising His works while you enjoy His creation. Maybe it's drawing, being creative, or listening to the sounds of your children as they sing and laugh.

SEEK GOD FIRST THROUGH REPETITION, DISCIPLINE, AND GRACE.

Hebrews 4:16 says, "Let us come boldly to the throne of our gracious God. There we will receive his mercy, and we

Prioritize His Presence

will find grace to help us when we need it most" (NLT). We have a High Priest who is not only strong but compassionate. The enemy wants us to see Him as unapproachable. But we can be bold in seeking God constantly, without reservation and with the utmost freedom. We can be bold in the persistent and constant grace of God.

My prayer is that these simple suggestions for how to seek God in your regular day-to-day will equip you with the tools you need to prioritize the presence of God in your life with grace. We can do a lot, but let's not forget that it's the kindness of God that does the most. It's the kindness of God that made a home in us, and it is that same kindness that keeps us tethered when we are so prone to wander. Our minds wander, we get distracted, and we become preoccupied by the presence of anything but Him. That's part of being human. Yet do not despair. Just keep coming back day after day. You will find that God is always there.

Today Is a New Day

You might be thinking, *Okay, Tara. I hear you. I get it. I need to prioritize the presence of God, but I'm tired. I don't have any more wiggle room in my energy or my schedule.* Did I nail your thoughts in this moment? You're not sure how much effort you can give to seeking God first when you wake up still exhausted from the day before. If that's you, I have some good news. Jesus doesn't demand your perfection. He just wants your presence. He just wants your presence in His presence. And in His presence we find the answers we're looking for, the strength we need, and the desire to live all in.

Jesus didn't say to come to Him only when you have it all together, feel 100 percent, or have a wide-open schedule. On the contrary! He said, "Come to me, all who labor and are heavy laden, and I will give you rest" (Matthew 11:28). So bring what you have to the feet of Jesus. Your exhaustion. Your distracted mind. Your desires. Your schedule. Your broken pieces. Your fears. Your hesitancies. Your reservations. Come.

There will be things God calls you to lay down, surrender, say "see you later" to for a season or maybe even "goodbye" to forever. You might even start noticing daily distractions that once felt harmless aren't doing your soul any favors, and you'll choose to let them go. That's where the work comes in. We all have the same number of hours in our day, but we must decide what we do with those hours.

Perhaps it would help us to shift our perspective to be closer to that of Brother Lawrence, a Carmelite monk in the 1600s who, after giving his life to God and leaving the army, spent his days doing grimy kitchen work and repairing sandals in a monastery. Let our prayers reflect his heart, even as tedious and grimy work filled his days.

Jesus doesn't demand your *perfection*. He just wants your *presence*.

Overbooked and Overwhelmed

My God, since You are with me, and since, by Your will, I must occupy myself with external things, please grant me the grace to remain with You, in Your presence. Work with me, so that my work might be the very best. Receive as an offering of love both my work and my affections.[3]

Prioritize His Presence

Reflection Questions

1. What are some simple yet practical ways you can prioritize the presence of God while you go about other tasks during your day?
2. Is there a desire within you to be productive? Is it possible that that desire could be negatively affecting your proximity to God and how much time you spend with Him?
3. How do you perceive God? Often when we forget He is kind, merciful, and gracious, we also forget how approachable He is and how deeply He desires our presence over perfection. Ask God to help you see Him for who He truly is.

SEVEN

The Power of Your Yes and No

Never is a woman so fulfilled as when she chooses to underwhelm her schedule so she can let God overwhelm her soul.
LYSA TERKEURST

*D*o you struggle with FOMO, the fear of missing out? We trivialize it and make jokes about it with its cutesy acronym, but let's just call it what it is: It's fear. It's our fear of what we may not get to experience, who we may disappoint, or what we won't achieve if we say no to opportunities that pop up. FOMO is a distraction in and of itself. It takes our eyes off living fully awake to life with Jesus, because we are afraid of what might happen if we miss what's going on around us. So we overbook and overcommit. We say yes to more than we should.

After physically and spiritually burning myself out, there was one life practice in particular that I knew God was calling me to do: start saying no. But that tiny, two-letter word felt anything but tiny. "No" felt like a cuss word. "Yes" felt like the right word, the God word, the loving word, the only word. So I refused the Spirit's call for a while, ignoring that gnawing feeling inside, and continued to say yes to just about everything and everyone.

Sadly, my obsession with saying yes did not come from a desire to honor God or put Him first. I overbooked, overcommitted, and overused the word "yes" because I was afraid of letting people down. I didn't realize it at the time, but my overuse of "yes" was my way of pleasing people and pleasing myself. I didn't want to miss out on any experience that came my way for fear of how I would be perceived or what I would not gain.

Overbooked and Overwhelmed

I don't know about you, but this mindset is easy for me to fall into as the holiday seasons come and go. In fact, as I write this chapter, I'm nursing a pulled chest muscle from coughing for the past month after getting that dreaded nasty cold that everyone seems to get every year. This holiday season has been the busiest one yet for our little family. For seven days in a row, we had a social obligation every day, sometimes with two events bookending the day.

The last event of our marathon week was supposed to be a progressive dinner with my parents and our family friends. A progressive dinner is an all-night event where you start at one family's house with appetizers, move to the next for the main course, and then end at the last house for dessert. That was the last box to check on our holiday schedule. Although we enjoyed every moment of the busy season, on the day of the progressive dinner, I was hanging on by a thread. As my body was saying no to our overbooked schedule, my brain was unrelenting.

Michael gently knocked on the bedroom door, holding Hunter in his arms after getting him up from bed, pj's and all. From the doorway, Michael looked at me with puppy-dog eyes and said, "I don't think we should go to the progressive dinner tonight, hon."

"But I don't want to miss out," I moaned, then coughed. Every fiber of my being was so set on going to this dinner that I had blocked out my body's clear warning signs. I needed rest and recovery. I took Michael's advice and eventually realized he was right. We needed to stay home and miss out, so we did. We missed out. And I was glad we did.

My guess is that you're no stranger to FOMO either—whether it's the fear of missing out on a party or a trip or even on a dream. Perhaps you have believed or are currently believing that saying yes all the time is just what you need to do. After all, your motivations are pure. You don't want to say no, because you love people, you want to serve, you want to be in community, or you want to be where the joy and excitement are. But your good intentions may just be wringing you out. Sooner or later, the effects of an unhealthy relationship with the words "yes" and "no" will catch up to you.

Our perception of the word "yes" may just be skewed. God does not ask us to wring ourselves out like a washcloth for His name. Rather, He discourages it. He reminds us that it's only through His grace that His power is made perfect in our weakness—in our noes, our inabilities, and our lack. The life we long for is found in spending our energy on the assignments, callings, and situations that are worth it. The life we long for is found in putting our focus on the God things.

What if instead we started having FOMO for the things of God—a desire to not miss out on what God has for us? What if we started allowing truth to dictate our actions from a place of Him being first in our lives? The good news is that in Christ we don't have to fear missing out. In Him, we have the fulfillment of everything we long for. Jesus is here, He's

Overbooked and Overwhelmed

alive in us, and He's not going anywhere. Yes, you and I will miss out on some things from an earthly perspective when Jesus is first in our lives. You can bet that Jesus will call you to say no to situations, pleasures, and more in order to be fully awake to what really matters—the eternal things. But if we choose to say no to lesser things in order to keep up with Him, there will be less room for us to miss our purpose. And maybe that's the kind of FOMO worth having, the kind that compels us to be so in sync with Jesus that we don't miss the abundant life He has for us, the abundant life that overwhelm wants to steal from us.

We want a life that is intentional, in the big and the small. We want a life that is less overwhelming and simpler. To get there, to choose the better portion, we have to make a choice. We can't let the fear of missing out distract us or fixate on the what-ifs when the Word of Life Himself is sitting in our living room waiting for us to slow down. The enemy of our souls wants to distract us with the desire to go all out—saying yes to the world and everything it has to offer—but what happens in the end? We become distracted from our purpose and from the One who gave that purpose to us. We grow so busy with our commitments, or overcommitments, that there's little margin left for our Savior and what He's called us to.

> *If we choose to say no to lesser things in order to keep up with Him, there will be less room for us to miss our purpose.*

Learning the way of intentional yeses and noes won't just help you in your day-to-day life. It will also help you keep God first as you stop giving in to the pressure to overbook or overcommit but, instead, intentionally choose what will draw you closer to God. Learning this way of life not only gives you peace from the overwhelm of your demanding schedule; it will also give you a surpassing peace in your home, body, and relationship with God.

Prayer, Hard Work, and Putting God First

One thing I love about God is how He will reveal the same truths in the Bible that we've learned before but in a new, refreshing light. Reading a verse or book of the Bible today feels worlds different for me now from how it did five years ago, not because the truth has changed but because I've changed. One of my new realizations is found in the book of Nehemiah. Tucked in between the books of Ezra and Esther, we read the tale of an ordinary man with an extraordinary purpose.

The name Nehemiah means "Yahweh comforted." (The name Tara means "hill" . . . lame.) Nehemiah's mission was to rebuild the ruined walls around Jerusalem and oversee hundreds of workers. His life teaches us that not only is it possible to put God first in the face of overwhelm, opposition, and distraction, but it is 1,000 percent worth it. Let's zoom in on the details of his life to learn how we, too, can overcome the temptations, circumstances, and overwhelm through fervent prayer, hard work, and prioritizing God no matter what.

DETAIL #1: NEHEMIAH KNEW THE VALUE OF HIS WORK AND HIS SIGNIFICANT CALLING.

> "I am doing a great work and I cannot come down. Why should the work stop while I leave it and come down to you?" (Nehemiah 6:3)

Growing up, I loved watching the Kentucky Derby. Unlike farm horses, Derby racehorses are dressed to the nines with all sorts of equipment, including blinders. These blinders are attached to the horses' heads and prevent them from seeing to the rear and the sides. The purpose of blinders is to keep the horses focused on what is in front of them, encouraging them to pay attention to the race instead of things that could distract them, like the crowds of people or other racers. Gosh, sometimes I wish I had blinders. It is too darn easy to get whisked away by distractions and forget what and Who I am really living for.

Nehemiah had not only his eyes but his heart set on what God had called him to, which was supervising the rebuilding of Jerusalem's walls. He had spiritual blinders on that allowed him to give his best effort to work with eternal significance, however menial it may have looked from the outside. Nehemiah's life shows us that living undistracted

The Power of Your Yes and No

and committed to God starts with realizing the greater significance of our Savior and our calling first.

When we don't put up spiritual blinders, we, like Derby horses, may get swayed off course. If we are not careful, earthly distractions like social media, entertainment, relationships, money, jobs, and school can take our eyes off eternity. Enjoy your social media accounts. Work hard. Watch a movie with your spouse. Eat a delicious dinner. Make money to support your family. But don't let those things become the reason you wake up every morning, the heart of your worship, or the place where you put your worth.

DETAIL #2: NEHEMIAH PRAYED DAILY FOR GOD'S WISDOM AND DISCERNMENT.

> "Let your ear be attentive and your eyes open, to hear the prayer of your servant that I now pray before you day and night for the people of Israel your servants." (Nehemiah 1:6)

My husband is my fierce prayer warrior. He will tell you that he naturally leans toward the introverted side of the scale, but he is loud and vocal with his prayers. There is value in consistent and constant prayer. That's something we see in Nehemiah too. Before speaking to the king, he prayed. Before he answered the king, he prayed. While he worked on the wall, he prayed. While he faced opposition, he prayed. When the noise and distractions and clamor of life were unrelenting, he prayed. Even when he had accomplished his goal and rebuilt the walls, he prayed.

Don't brush this off. Here's what made Nehemiah's prayers powerful: Not only was he praying in any and every situation, but his prayers were ripe with wisdom and discernment. In the face of adversity, confusion, overwhelm, and fear, he petitioned and pleaded with God to show him what mattered and what didn't matter.

Oftentimes, we want God to reveal things to us and give us wisdom on how to live better, but we're not asking Him for revelation or wisdom. We will never have the wisdom or discernment required to arrive at our most intentional yes and no if we are not asking God for it in prayer.

DETAIL #3: NEHEMIAH DIDN'T GIVE IN TO HIS ENEMY. HE HELD THE LINE.

"They sent to me four times in this way, and I answered them in the same manner." (Nehemiah 6:4)

Tobiah and Sanballat were Nehemiah's nemeses when it came to rebuilding the wall, not to mention annoying. Their jabs, taunts, and attempts to ruin God's work were relentless. We learn later that they sent messengers to dissuade Nehemiah not four times but five—and that time with a passive-aggressive letter. But what was Nehemiah's response? He pressed in even harder to the call of God. He said yes to God and no to his enemies.

The truth is that people will criticize you at some point

The Power of Your Yes and No

in your life. People will make fun of you for the choices you make. They won't understand why you say yes and no to the things that you do. They will accuse you of being too uptight and tell you to loosen up. So when that time comes, remember that you don't need to say yes to the things that everyone else is doing for the sake of being relevant or liked or approved. You're accountable to give your yes only to the One who called you to build, just like Nehemiah. You are here to please God, not man.

Yes, you're here to love people, but true godly love does not give in to the fear of man. Nehemiah did not go on the offensive and attack his enemies after they sent their messengers armed with falsities. Nor did he slander them with gossip or grow hard in his heart. Instead he responded with firm truth, secure in the fact that if God was faithful to call him to this work—however hard it might be—God would complete it. He would bring it all to pass. It would be worth it. And it was.

DETAIL #4: NEHEMIAH RELIED ON GOD'S STRENGTH.

"Now, O God, strengthen my hands." (Nehemiah 6:9)

It's easy to read all of this and conclude that Nehemiah was the perfect example. But we know that there's no such thing as a perfect person this side of eternity. You can bet that Nehemiah had his moments of discouragement, overwhelm, and stress while looking at his workload and responsibilities.

But that wasn't the main part of his story. Spoiler alert: It doesn't have to be ours either.

After responding to his enemies, Nehemiah prayed once again that God would strengthen his hands. In order to keep giving God his best yes, he needed God's strength. He needed the grace, blessing, and kindness of Jehovah-jireh to breathe life into an extremely trying circumstance. Making sure that we don't miss out on the things of God requires a humble heart that petitions the throne of heaven for supernatural strength—mentally, physically, emotionally, and spiritually.

DETAIL #5: NEHEMIAH HONORED OTHER PEOPLE WELL AND ASKED FOR HELP.

"We all returned to the wall, each to his work."
(Nehemiah 4:15)

When the wall was finally finished, it wasn't solely because of Nehemiah. He wasn't intent on proving something from a desire of doing it all on his own. He had an army of men. He didn't take on God's call and assignment by himself.

Nothing worthwhile or significant, let alone eternal, is built alone. I'm preaching to my soul first with this lesson. Asking for help once felt like dying to me. It was really my arrogance and pride that blinded me from two of God's greatest gifts: relationship and community with others. But through circumstances like my health struggles and motherhood, God has taught me the beauty of help.

A hard-heartedness to do things on our own often stems from a place of wanting to receive all the glory, honor, and recognition. But a tender meek-heartedness that humbly invites other people into our daily lives stems from a place of knowing that fulfilling God's call includes community.

Limitations Are Liberating

One of my proudest adulting moments was when I opened my LLC. A few years after I first met with my accountant, he encouraged me to make my ministry business official. It was a big, serious step in my professional life. I felt like an adult, opening a business checking account and receiving a shiny new credit card for business purchases and expenses. As I continued to faithfully steward that account, I started to get letters in the mail from my bank notifying me that my credit card limit had gone up. Before I knew it, my limit had tripled. As I stared at that large number, I recalled some of the financial wisdom I had heard from people like my parents and my personal finance teacher in high school: *Never spend beyond your limits*, and *Just because you have a high credit card limit does not mean you need to reach that limit.*

With phrases like "Max out your potential" and "Get past your limiting beliefs," we've grown to believe that having restraints, limits, and restrictions is weak. And before we know it, those beliefs cause us to live for the thrill of pushing the boundaries and doing it all. But Jesus didn't preach sermons on how to reach higher. He preached sermons on how to be like a child. To His disciples and the crowds around Him, children were often considered a distraction. They were viewed as some of the lowest-ranking and least consequential members of society. That's what makes Jesus' words in Mark 10:14 so jaw-dropping: "Let the little children come to me, and do not hinder them, for the kingdom of God belongs to such as these" (NIV). Usually when we read this passage, we think about the childlike faith Jesus refers to as simple and free and trusting without reservation. But what if there's another part we've been missing? What if this verse also speaks to the limitations we often resist and how those limitations can actually work for our good?

Little children have countless limitations. I don't have to look far to find a very personal example of this. All I have to do is lock eyes with my little boy. Hunter can't yet reach the toilet by himself to go to the bathroom. He can't yet verbalize the deep emotions he feels inside. He can't yet make his own food. He can't quite make it through the day without a nap. Yet, for the most part, those limitations only push him further into dependence on Michael and me as his parents. His childlike deficiencies put him in the perfect place to rely on us and trust us fully.

Limitations, if seen through the lens of Christ, are liberating. They push us toward God's strength when we come to the end of ours. And they are license to give two of life's most precious commodities—time and energy—to the things of God. To the things that matter. Leaning in to our limitations

Limitations are liberating. They push us toward God's strength when we come to the end of ours.

and leveraging our most intentional yeses and noes keep us stayed on course for our lives.

Like David said in Psalm 90:12, "Teach us to realize the brevity of life, so that we may grow in wisdom" (NLT). Realizing the brevity of life, or learning the extent of our limitations, gives us the ability to make the most of our days, since they really are so few. Only through prayer and dependence on God can we gain a heart of wisdom, and only from that heart of wisdom are we able to say yes to the God things and no to the wrong things.

Take heart, my friend. God knows your frame. God knows your limitations. God created you this way. He did this not to stifle your creativity, rob you of your purpose, or withhold satisfaction but to give you the space to live undistracted, wholeheartedly devoted to His purposes that ultimately bring you the most creativity, the most purpose, and the deepest satisfaction. Use each limitation—each circumstance you are called to say no to—as an invitation to spend more time in His presence. In His presence, there is fullness of joy (Psalm 16:11).

Reflection Questions

1. Is there something that God is calling you to say no to for a season or forever?
2. What limitations are you experiencing right now? How might those limitations be freeing to you, and how can you depend on God more in those weaknesses?
3. Is there one example from Nehemiah's life you want to emulate in your life this week?

EIGHT

A Word for the Weary

Resilience isn't about sheer strength, and it's not about stubborn persistence either. Resilience is faithful perseverance.

REBEKAH LYONS

*O*n a random day in March, I woke up with an irresistible urge to overhaul our front yard and spruce up the landscaping of our rental home. Nothing fancy or expensive, just something nicer than plain ol' dirt. Perhaps some perennials, annuals, and a few of the other -als. I texted my mom, the one I knew could help me execute my vision. (In another life I bet she would have been a florist or opened her own nursery.) The next week my mom and I spent a few hours gallivanting through rows and rows of flowers, bushes, and shrubs at a local plant nursery. As an early Mother's Day gift, she bought me a few trays of flowers she thought were low maintenance, yet beautiful.

The two of us played in the dirt for the next hour, casting vision over where each plant would go. Trowels in hand, we dug our holes, sprinkled in some fertilizer, and nestled the plants in their resting places. Grinning, I scanned my front yard with pride. It wasn't much, but it was lovely. It wasn't much, but it was doable. My mom had helped me choose some of the most resilient plants. Surely I could keep these plants happy, alive, and thriving. Or so I thought.

For the next two weeks, I was faithfully devoted to watering my plants. I got into a routine of watering them after Hunter went to bed. With the prolonged summer sunlight, I happily skipped around my front yard with my garden hose. *I'm nailing this.* But as our schedule got busier, fatigue from life set in, and as the initial excitement wore off, my watering routine relaxed. I watered my plants five times a week . . . three times a week . . . one time a week . . . and then not at all.

Months later, the weatherman forecast a week of scorching temperatures. After putting Hunter to bed, I dragged myself off the couch, away from the air-conditioning, and outside to check on my plants. Unraveling the hose from the reel, I wandered over to the first plant. I looked down. It was drier than the desert. *Oops*. I moved to the next plant. *Yikes*. And the next and the next. Every single plant, its leaves once green and its flower petals in bloom, had shriveled up. I cringed but decided to give the plants a good shot of water anyway. I had high hopes that, with one day of excessive watering, my plants would return to their budding state overnight.

The next day I darted through the yard with anticipation. My face fell. My plants were just as I had left them the night before. Desiccated. Shriveled. Depleted. Parched. Beyond saving. At first I chalked it up to the excessive heat we were experiencing that summer. Sure, that was definitely a contributing factor. But I had to come to terms with the reality that my plants hadn't thrived and flourished because I did not weed and water them continually. I did not tend to their needs on a regular basis. I was not consistent with my care.

The same was true of my walk with God during that season. I felt dry. Depleted. Idle. At a standstill. The Bible felt less than alive to me. My desire to pray was less than zero. I was just coasting and drifting through life. I talked a big talk in public. I posted things, encouraged my friends, and counseled others in the truth of God's Word with a smile on my face, but on the inside languished a barren and parched heart. Just like my plants, my heart had been choked out by my environment.

As with a math problem or science project, there are cause-and-effect equations in life. In mathematics, the cause-and-effect relationship is defined as a change in X producing a change in Y. Causes precede effects, not the other way around. One thing affects the other. This principle played out in my life in a soul-deep way. That season of spiritual dryness and carelessness came about when I was at my most soul distracted. I didn't just feel disconnected from God; I felt disinterested in having a relationship with God. Why? Because I allowed distractions and overwhelming situations to overcome me. The more I set my gaze on worldly things and distractions, the less I desired to look in the eyes of my Savior.

> **X (cause/root) = I set my gaze on worldly things and distractions for fulfillment and enjoyment.**
> **Y (effect/result) = I grew more and more indifferent to God and cultivating a relationship with Him.**

The effort we put into our relationship with God, whether it's a great effort, little effort, or no effort, will produce something. Our input determines our output. When we struggle with soul distraction and put things above Jesus, our relationship with Him suffers. It's a spiritual equation. When other things become bigger than Him, our souls bear the weight. And we shouldn't be surprised when we feel the nagging sensation of spiritual depletion or stagnancy.

Distraction opens the door to distancing ourselves from God, distance opens the door to disconnecting ourselves from God, and disconnection opens the door to complete soul overwhelm. This is a matter to be taken seriously. Not because we feel like we ought to take it seriously, but because it's a matter of our spiritual formation. It's a matter of our souls. And our souls matter greatly to God.

Cling to this truth as we walk through the rest of this chapter and let it bring you hope: "You will seek me and find me, when you seek me with all your heart" (Jeremiah 29:13).

When Life Chokes You Out

One of my least favorite tasks growing up was weeding at my dad's hazelnut nursery. I hated it with every fiber of my being. Weeding felt inconsequential, tedious, and, frankly, unimportant. I would have much preferred manning a tractor, pruning tender shoots, or moving pipe (which is saying a lot). But at least once a month, my brother, cousins, and I were tasked with weeding an entire greenhouse of baby hazelnut trees. These trees were spoken for by local farmers who would soon plant them on their properties, so we had to take good care of them.

A Word for the Weary

Some weeds were easy to uproot, flimsy and superficial at best. But others would take a little more elbow grease. My farming father stressed how important it was to pull a weed up from its roots. It wasn't enough to pull off the head or *mostly* all of it. The only way to get rid of it for good and to care for the tree was to grab ahold of the weed at its base and remove its roots (its life source). Otherwise the weed would keep growing and would eventually overtake the tree.

Whenever I think about how we weeded the hazelnut trees, I also think of Matthew 13, where Jesus told the parable of the seed sower. In the parable He compared four different environments that seeds might be planted in to four different heart postures that people might have, illustrating how receptive (or unreceptive) people are to the Word of God. In verse 22 Jesus said, "As for what was sown among thorns, this is the one who hears the word, but the cares of the world and the deceitfulness of his riches choke the word, and it proves unfruitful."

Just as a weed affects the health of a hazelnut tree, so the things of this world affect our relationship with God. A plant left unattended suffers. A plant left neglected, allowing weeds to overtake it, becomes compromised. Its growth suffers. Jesus' main message concealed in a story about a choked-out seed was to illustrate what happens to a life, a soul, and a heart when the world becomes greater than Him. This seed was weighed down by the cares of this world—riches, worries, stress, comparison, hardship—and those things hindered the seed from flourishing.

Overbooked and Overwhelmed

The same thing can happen to us. Some of us feel spiritually dry and numb today because of physical, mental, or emotional pain. It can be hard to get out of bed and get through the day, let alone focus for a few moments in the Word. For others—like those in the early days of motherhood—it's a fight to even shower or find two minutes to yourself, let alone put in the effort to maintain a relationship with God on a daily basis. Sadly, spiritual dryness and the difficulties that come with it are often par for the course when it comes to spiritual life on earth, because we are imperfect people on an imperfect planet.

I wonder whether you, too, are walking through a season where life feels like it is choking you out like weeds. The responsibilities are endless, and people are constantly looking to you. There's so much to do, and because of that you're left with a heart crushed and weighed down by the cares of the world. This choking? It's exhausting, to say the least. It's struggle after struggle. Now, your heart may be in the right place—you want fruitful soil for God to cultivate—and yet the overwhelming circumstances and situations that arise each day squeeze the joy, purpose, and energy out of your soul. My friend, you're not alone. I lived in that barren season for so long. I allowed the thorns to take over the soil of my life, the soil that was meant to produce beautiful fruit.

I know you're feeling pressed on every side right now, so can I give you some hope? You do not always have to be a victim to the thorns and the cares of this world. You are not a helpless bystander. You may be discouraged by a lack of spiritual growth and a lack of motivation to pursue your faith these days, but the fact that you are still here means that God is not finished. His mercies are new every morning (Lamentations 3:22), which means that His mercies never run out. His well never runs dry.

The cares of this world may be surrounding you, but the good news is that Jesus Christ can break any chain. He overcame the cross for you, so that you could overcome whatever is in your way or whatever is robbing you of living on fire. Even at your driest, most distressed, and most stuck, there is a Good Shepherd and Gardener who will bring you back to life.

Hope for Your Weary Wilderness

Some girls are camping girls and others are glamping girls. I'm proudly the latter. A perfect example of my being a glamping girl is a story from when I was seventeen. It was Michael's family reunion, and I was invited to tag along. Because we weren't married at the time, his grandparents offered their pull-out couch to me in their fancy-schmancy RV. I was living the life—my phone plugged in and never without charge, a cozy bed, and the coffeepot set to start brewing when I woke up (thanks, Papa Jerry). To this day I am teased relentlessly about how that wasn't real camping, because I wasn't sleeping in a tent or going to the bathroom in a hole. Oh well. I didn't care.

Overbooked and Overwhelmed

Although life is much busier these days, Michael will still find the occasional weekend to go camping with his family, more so to go hunting than camping, though. I happily help him pack and send him off with food for the weekend like a doting wife. I mean, the mere thought of no showers or porcelain thrones alone is enough to keep me away. But what Michael enjoys about hunting isn't necessarily whether he shoots a buck or not (although that's always preferred); it's the serenity of hunting. The stillness, the quiet, and being way out in the wilderness shift his perspective. Any hunter, from novice to expert, knows that the wilderness is the place to be.

The men that God used to write Scripture knew the power of the wilderness too. They wrote of wilderness encounters from the Israelites' forty years of wandering to Jesus' temptation, and there is one thing each of those encounters in the Bible has in common: The wilderness was a place where God's people were drawn into deeper relationship with God Himself. It wasn't just a physical location. It was a place of spiritual transformation. It was a divine locale that God used to draw His people into a heightened experience and revival when they needed it most.

Imagine wandering in the wilderness for forty years like the Israelites. Imagine not just wandering but living, eating, sleeping, and raising children in the wilderness. Imagine just how many questions, doubts, and fears they had. Imagine how pessimistic they must have grown about the promises of God. We see their grumblings, their complaints, and their dwindling optimism in Exodus. But, greater still, we see God's provision.

In Exodus 15 the Israelites weren't just physically parched after going three days without water. They were spiritually parched too. They were dwelling on their circumstances, giving in to discouragement, growing bitter toward God, and distracting themselves with temporary idols. But what did God do? He made the bitter water, their only source of water in the wilderness, sweet and satisfying.

Now, look to Jesus' wilderness experience. There is a stark contrast between how Jesus navigated His wilderness and how the Israelites navigated theirs. Both were spiritually challenging, dry, and testing locations. Whereas the Israelites allowed their spiritually weary souls to succumb to distrust and forgetfulness, Jesus pressed in. He allowed barren wasteland to lead Him into a deeper, and more fulfilling, relationship with His heavenly Father. Matthew 4 tells us that the Holy Spirit led Jesus into the wilderness to be tempted by the enemy, Satan. This wasn't a punishment or a bait-and-switch situation. No, this was a divine test.

Matthew 4:2–3 says, "After fasting forty days and forty nights, he was hungry. And the tempter came and said to him, 'If you are the Son of God, command these stones to become loaves of bread.'" The enemy hit Jesus where it hurt the most. After forty days without food, He was starving. With a gnarly right hook, the enemy swung. He taunted Jesus to create food out of stones. Then he taunted Jesus to throw Himself off the highest point of the temple to prove

He was the Savior. And finally, the enemy taunted Jesus to bow down at his feet and worship him. But Jesus didn't take Satan's blows lying down, and He certainly didn't waver. With every test, He answered with a promise from God's Word.

This is our example; this is our blueprint. This is the first step we must take in our most distracted, stuck, and spiritually stagnant seasons. The enemy would love to deprive us of feeling God's presence and love in the wilderness, but the Lord wants to—and will—strengthen us in the wilderness by replacing the discouragement we feel with His hope, His son, Jesus.

You might be thinking, *Tara, I feel so spiritually stuck and worn out. Fighting for truth and coming to Jesus require energy that I don't have to give.* Adding yet another thing to do when you're already depleted is exhausting. Your schedule is already overbooked, and your mind is too overstimulated to think about doing yet another thing. I hear you, so hear me: You don't have to go very far.

With every one step we take toward Jesus, He takes a million leaps toward us. With every feeble attempt we make to drag ourselves forward, He shows His strength in pursuing us first. Jesus is not disgusted by our lack of energy or follow-through. He is merciful and gracious. So what I need you to know is that all it takes is one step, or one

> God desires for those wilderness seasons to shape us by elevating our awareness of Him and deepening our dependence on Him.

stumble if you're feeling exhausted like me, to fall into the depths of His revival. And as we experience more and more of that refreshment, it makes coming back all the sweeter and more achievable.

This is a war cry against spiritual apathy and a march toward spiritual grit. When hard times come and when we become overbooked and overwhelmed, the answer isn't to admit defeat and let the wilderness season win. The answer is to lean in to how God desires for those wilderness seasons to shape us by elevating our awareness of Him and deepening our dependence on Him.

A Road Map for Rehydrating Our Souls

But what is that one step that we should take next? How do we revive our souls in Jesus and put guardrails in place to ensure that the cares of this world do not rob us of what matters most? We need a practical and biblical road map for what to do when we find ourselves overstimulated by the world and underwhelmed by our faith. Here are just a few ideas to consider.

REMEMBER AND REFLECT.

Ask yourself these questions, and give yourself honest answers:

- Where have I been that I am grateful for as I look back?
- Where do I want to be now?
- What is going to get me there?

If you're in a stagnant or stuck season in your faith, remember a time in your life when you were on fire. Remembrance is not only a powerful mental tool but a powerful biblical tool that causes us to reflect. Oftentimes, we allow ourselves to be so overwhelmed by what's in front of us that we cannot sit comfortably in a quiet moment of reflection and remembrance. Look introspectively, but always look biblically as well. Remember and refresh yourself with the scriptures and gospel truths that brought you to Jesus in the first place.

Next, look to where you want to be. Where do you want to be in your Bible reading, your prayer time, and your prioritization of Jesus? There's something not only healthy and holy but also scientifically proven about the power of goals and partnering with God to get where you desire to be next.

And, lastly, get practical. What is going to get you to the life you long for? Think about what needs to be uprooted in order for you to reclaim the relationship with God you want, and then consider what people or resources you can tap into that will help you get there.

TURN A NEW WAY.

Repentance is described as a 180-degree turn, a turning from one direction and going a new way. If you've been going the opposite way of the life Jesus longs for you to have, know that plain in His Word is the instruction for how to repent, confess, and turn onto a better, more life-giving path. Acknowledge your struggle, repent of the idleness, and shake off the shame so you can walk in new light. We can't walk in revival if we're stuck following the same old path.

DON'T ACT LIKE YOU HAVE IT ALL TOGETHER.

Can I tell you a secret? No one is under the assumption that life isn't hard and that being a Christian isn't sometimes difficult. Shed the false narrative that you can't admit the struggle to your loved ones and to God. Spoiler alert: He already knows, but He wants your communication. For Christians, admission is a powerful tool that frees us from shame and propels us into grace and sanctification—the process of God forming us more and more into the image of His Son. This is actually where freedom begins. You're in good company.

DRAW ON SOMETHING NEW.

Even the most type A, routine-oriented of us can benefit from something new. Think about it. A car left unused for months has a hard time turning over. A piece of bread left out on the counter for weeks will grow stale and moldy. Switch it up. Try something new. Sometimes the simplest of switches can give us refreshment—not only in our routines but in our souls. Break out of the old and break out of the mold.

Buy a new Bible or try reading in a different location.

Listen to an audio Bible for a while. Journal your prayers instead of speaking them out loud. Try putting your phone in a different room overnight and replacing it with a good ol'-fashioned alarm clock.

Results That Stick

When I was diagnosed with fibromyalgia at fourteen, one of the steps in my rigorous recovery routine was physical exercise. I rolled my eyes at my doctor and reminded him that I was a ballet dancer and had been physically active since I was four. But what I didn't want to admit was that fibromyalgia had drastically affected my physical state. My doctor explained that I needed more physical exercise, specifically strength training.

So on the days I was not in the dance studio, I worked out with a personal trainer, Bridget. Her workouts were tough and intense, but her heart was soft and kind. She tailored my workout regimen to be in line with my doctor's orders to build more muscular endurance and strength. Holding a perfect ballet penché or a relevé en pointe is legit but so is squatting with two twenty-pound dumbbells racked on your shoulders.

Research has concluded that physical activity is one of the best ways to manage fibromyalgia symptoms.[1] What changed the game for me in my chronic-illness journey was building a real vision for the long term. Adding weightlifting and strength training to what I was already doing wasn't about toughening up in the temporary. In order to learn how to live with fibromyalgia for the foreseeable future, I needed something more than a quick fix to get me through. I needed true, physical resilience, a strengthening that would last.

It took a good four weeks to settle into my new, rigorous workout routine. On Mondays, Wednesdays, and Thursdays, I moved my body in a leotard and ballet shoes. And on Tuesdays and Fridays, I moved my body in leggings and training sneakers. There were days when I wanted to throw in the towel. There were days when I wanted to succumb to the warmth of my bed and shoot a text to my trainer telling her I wasn't going to come that day. But God gave me the supernatural foresight and vision to push through the temporary struggle, and after four weeks, returning to the gym and the studio became not only more of a habit but also more of a joy.

It's the same for you and me when it comes to our relationship with God, especially in the dry seasons. The goal isn't merely to be tough in the temporary. The goal is to be resilient in daily rhythms, because that is the key to building a foundation that stands not only the test of time but the temptations of life. Seasons of dryness and apathy in our faith are unavoidable, but that doesn't mean we cannot overcome them. We must recognize our neediness as necessary and develop resilience.

Secular culture and social media do a poor job at teaching resilience and perseverance. Flashy six-second Instagram

The goal isn't merely to be tough in the temporary. The goal is to be resilient in daily rhythms.

A Word for the Weary

reels train our minds to move on quickly and diminish our focus for the long term. Shortcuts, quick fixes, and snappy hacks have taught us that the fastest way out is the best way through. But the kingdom of God operates in a more life-giving way—by teaching us how to press in to temporary discomfort, press past temporary distractions, and press on to eternal glory.

The spiritual muscle of resilience is one we must train in preparation for those times of spiritual dryness and numbness. When we don't feel like reading our Bible. When we don't want to pray. When we feel no desire to act on our faith. And certainly when we feel lifeless and stuck due to the distractions that have created so much distance between us and God.

How do we train that muscle so it's ready when the dry seasons come? While watching the summer Olympic Games, I discovered something interesting. A reporter asked members of the US women's gymnastics team what it was like training for such an event. One of the gymnasts laughed and went on to explain how it was really about "going all out." You see, when gymnasts approach the vault or uneven bars for their routine, they put themselves in danger if they are not committed to completing their moves at max capacity. They can't just do a triple backflip halfway—that would end in them falling on their face or getting fitted for a back brace. Instead, they have to go all out. In training, this means loading up weight until you can't anymore, which builds greater tension and, as a result, leads to greater strength and resilience. Then, when they get to the event, they continue going all out by doing all the stretches and warm-ups with excellence before then nailing a perfect routine at the Olympics.

In the same way, if we're going to build up our spiritual muscle of resilience, we need to go all out and go all in with Jesus. We need to strive for excellence and consistency in both the big things (an Olympic routine) and the small things (daily stretching and conditioning). As Russell from the beloved Pixar movie *Up* says, "I think the boring stuff is the stuff I remember the most."[2] There is power in showing up every single day. There is power in not despising the small things. There is power in diligent work that feels small but in reality is building a powerhouse inside you.

Train yourself in the Word of God each day, even if that looks like just five minutes at first. Be humble enough to ask others to journey with you. Remember to treasure what God says more than what your mind may be telling you in the temporary. In the thick of it, preach to yourself that this season is just that—a season.

The reality is that there will be seasons of wilderness when we abandon our first love, like the church at Ephesus did when John rebuked them in the book of Revelation (2:1–7). They knew their doctrine and the Scriptures, but life was no longer a daily love story with Christ. Their perspective of eternity, the grandness of their calling, and the greatness of God fell out of focus. The Ephesians knew the Word, but along the way, they fell away from a true, loving relationship. This is a danger we all will face.

There will be times when thorns grow up in our lives, the sun beats down on our backs, and the enemy capitalizes on hard circumstances. But there is a glimmer of gospel hope that pervades it all: God loves us with the fiercest, most committed, most consistent love. If you find yourself stuck or overwhelmed, choked by hardships and burned by life, look up. Look to His love. Shake loose the dirt and dust that have been collecting. Stir up your soul with a reminder of what it's really longing for: love. A love that refreshes, revives, and rescues.

Reflection Questions

1. Have you experienced a dry season in your faith, when you felt distant from God and stagnant in your growth? How did it feel, and were there any circumstances or situations that contributed to that season?
2. What promises or verses from God's Word can you hold on to when you feel distant and stuck in your faith?
3. In what ways can you work on growing spiritual resiliency? Name a few tangible ways you can start putting down roots now so you're better prepared when the wilderness seasons come.

NINE

More Rhythm, Less Rush

*Solitude with God repairs the damage done by
the fret and noise and clamor of the world.*
OSWALD CHAMBERS

*O*nce upon a time, just before my sophomore year of high school, a few of my friends convinced me to try cross-country summer camp. I was desperate for community and decided to try my hand at long-distance running, naively believing it would be a breeze because I was in such good shape from dance. Boy, oh boy, was I wrong. I quickly learned that long-distance running required a different kind of strength and training from dance.

When I got home that first night, my parents asked me how it went. My timid excuse was that it just wasn't for me when, in all reality, I could have applied myself, trained, and become a decent long-distance runner. But I didn't want to slow down or put in the hours, weeks, and months to get there.

My brief cross-country career was not my only experience with running. In middle school, just years prior, I had found a love for sprinting. The 100-meter and 200-meter races, to be exact. Unlike cross-country, the thrill of going fast lit me up. My quickest 100-meter time was just shy of ten seconds, which felt pretty close to flying. Maybe the reason why I loved sprinting so much was because it felt an awful lot like my preferred pace of life: fast.

Now in adulthood, I've been unironically called "Dash" from *The Incredibles* because of how quickly I complete tasks, get things done, and produce results. Most of my life has been lived in the fast lane, as the Eagles rock band would say. The Type A achiever in me loves going, going, going. So when the idea of hustle culture and living a high-paced life first emerged, it didn't take long for me to get hooked. I had been told that overworking, burning out, and running at a breakneck speed were unhealthy, but I didn't know why people said that. Hustle culture, intense productivity, and the continual strife excited me like nothing else. Every day was a race against my to-do list and a challenge to see how much I could accomplish, even in my free time. Whereas some people would look at a free day on their calendar as a blessing, I would frantically seek to fill it up with as much as possible.

Doing, accomplishing, and remaining busy felt like the epitome of my calling. I felt like I was fully myself and fully centered in God's will when I was overworking, over-accomplishing, and overbooking. But now, as I look back, I realize that I had taken a bite out of Eden's apple and listened to the enemy's lies. I believed his whispers, telling me that my greatest priority in life was to be busy. I learned the hard way that buying into this lie wasn't helping my relationship with God. I learned the hard way that I might have been busy but I sure wasn't busy for the right reasons. For the God reasons.

Even Olympic sprinters know that you can run at your top speed for only a certain amount of time until you start slowing and eventually stop. Sprinting is just not sustainable for a long period of time. Not even Usain Bolt, the Olympic champion once deemed the fastest man in the world, could run at his top speed forever with the same efficiency.

The obsession I had with doing and living life at top speed became a hindrance to my relationship with God, stifling my ability to live all in for Him when I was too busy to give Him the time He really deserved. In the end, I was left with a much more serious problem: I was not operating at Jesus' speed.

Spiritual Burnout

Most of us don't notice we're burned out until it's too late or we're quite far down that road. It's not that there aren't warning signs along the way, but I would guess that most of us are too busy and preoccupied to notice them before it's too late. Cleveland Clinic notes that "burnout also happens when your work-life balance is out of sync." The result of burnout often looks like a desire to disengage from life, a lack of emotion, or a desire to give up altogether due to weariness.[1] This is a weariness I've felt deeply.

After *Surrender Your Story* launched into the world, I had countless friends and family ask me what surprised me most about the publishing process. Most of them chuckled and said, "It was probably writing a two-hundred-page book, right?" While the writing itself was hard work, what surprised me the most was everything that came after that: months of edits, marketing calls, social media strategy, content calendar creation, sales calls, and press interviews. Now, I don't think that those things on their own were the cause of my eventual physical depletion, mental fatigue, or apathy toward life. What burned me out was my lack of boundaries, rest, and regular time in the presence of God to keep me grounded *while* I did those things.

Burnout wasn't the result of my busyness. Burnout was the result of my putting God on the back burner and not allowing Him to sustain me. When I was in the middle of burning out, completing my to-do list and hitting deadlines became more important and worthier of my time than sitting at the feet of Jesus. Whenever I had a free moment, all I could think of was what I could accomplish—or, in other words, what I could prove to myself and to the world.

Because God was not in the right place on my priority list, I did not know how to rightly handle life, so I spiraled into unhealthy rhythms and abandoned the pace of Jesus. Jess Connolly has taught me so much about this. She wrote, "Spiritual exhaustion may have set in if you're living in a have-to versus a get-to mentality about spiritual rhythms. You may also be spiritually tired if you've stopped seeing and seeking abundance and have instead begun only to operate out of obligation."[2] She's right. Spiritual burnout is a result of our forgetfulness of God's

More Rhythm, Less Rush

grace and His pace. It's the result of ignoring the gospel: Jesus saved us on that cross and there's nothing we can achieve or do to add to that.

While I knew this to be true, because I had entertained the idol of busyness for so long, I couldn't shut off the noise of my to-do list, even as I lay with Hunter on the floor while he batted at his playmat. I couldn't squash the feeling that I was falling behind when I nursed him on the couch. For the first time in my life, I fell victim to anxiety and panic attacks around dinnertime with Michael, in the car by myself, and at one in the morning in bed. My poor husband got my snide remarks, subtle jabs, and snarky arguments, because I had been burning the candle at both ends. How had I let things get this bad? The thing is that achievement, productivity, and busyness gave me an addicting sense of accomplishment and worth—what I imagine a high feels like. I didn't realize I was suffering spiritual burnout, because the sensation of achievement felt so great.

One of Satan's tactics throughout Scripture is to get God's people to forget what He has said and promised. When that happens, it's easier for the enemy to convince them they continually need to do more and to be more. Yet Jesus reminds us in John 10:10 that "the thief comes only to steal and kill and destroy. I came that they may have life and have it abundantly." In Greek, the word for "abundance" is *perissos*, which describes a surplus of something, with rich mathematical meaning. The pursuit of abundant life does not mean a surplus of hurry or overbooked souls. No, it is a powerful reminder that Jesus alone supplies our every need, and He has opened the doorway to a rich and full life. This full life was designed to be overflowing with meaningful activities that keep us tethered to Christ and on course with our mission.

The truth is, you and I were born into a broken world with broken messages of anxiety and hurry, but we don't have to conform to these messages. We get to conform to the image of Christ, the same Christ who didn't live a frenzied, spread-thin, burned-out life. We get to live by a less burdensome way of life. We get to receive the meaning, peace, purpose, and freedom Christ brings when we rest in the work He has already done on the cross, instead of trying to do it all ourselves.

John Mark Comer summed up the way I felt so perfectly when I was on the path to burning out: "You feel disconnected from God, others, and your own soul. On those rare times when you actually stop to pray (and by pray I don't mean ask God for stuff; I mean sit with God in the quiet), you're so stressed and distracted that your mind can't settle down long enough to enjoy the Father's company."[3]

I'm not the only one, right?

Friend, I know that you long for a life full of fulfilling, meaningful work that doesn't feel like spinning your wheels in anxious toil. You long for fewer seasons of burnout and overwhelm, for a peaceful, more rhythmic way of life. You long for a more doable way to handle all the things on your plate and an anchoring foundation to ground yourself to when life inevitably gets overwhelming. I know you want that, because that's what you were created for. You want your life to matter, and you want to achieve something great. I want that too. But in order for you and me to have that, we need to focus on what will get us there.

What will get us to that life we long for is not allowing busyness to be a distraction but reminding ourselves to slow down enough to see the surpassing beauty of Jesus. The life we long for is found when we commit to not living so busy and frantic that we rush past Him and miss Him in our moments. The pathway to eternal success is ensuring that we live with more rhythms and less rush. And when we do that, we'll be able to run with endurance at Jesus' pace and find that our days are far more life-giving and less overwhelming.

You Can't Savor Without Slowing

Our little Hunter is never without a smile on his face and energy pulsing through his veins. I swear he is always running, jumping, galloping, racing, or drifting like a race car around the room, Lightning McQueen–style. Life is a whole lot sweeter and a heck of a lot more fun with him in it.

This one time, we went on a family vacation with my parents and brother. Standing on our cabin's back patio, there were stunning trees and land as far as the eye could see. As an experiment, we let Hunter explore beyond the bounds of the property to see how far he would go before turning around and coming back to us. We always had our eyes on him but were shocked when he took off running, sensing the freedom that came when we didn't call or drag him back immediately.

With every stride, he picked up more and more speed. But after covering some serious ground, he stopped. He realized how far he had run from us. He cried out "Mama!" with tears and horror in his eyes. My guess is that he got so caught up in the moment, the thrill of speed, and the excitement of something new that he didn't notice just how far he had gotten away from his parents. He came crying, running, and tumbling back to the patio. He jumped into my lap and clutched my neck with no plans of letting go anytime soon.

This ordinary instance showed me something extraordinary about God. When we run too fast through life, our awareness of God and our nearness to Him are drastically reduced. Hunter was so occupied with running fast that, for a moment, it caused him to forget about the safety of his parents' presence. Because he ran so fast, the distance between him and us broadened, and in the end, that affected him deeply.

Just like Hunter, when you and I run too quickly through life, the landscape around us begins to blur. It's not the landscape that changes; it's our perception of that landscape. The speed of busyness obscures our view. We lose sight of Jesus' true beauty all around us, because we are so focused on what's ahead, the next big thing. But if we slow down or even stop to check out all that God is doing, we get to experience Him fully. When we slow down, we start living at Jesus' speed.

A Jesus Speed

Jesus' ministry on earth lasted three years. To some, Jesus' age at the launch of His ministry, at thirty, feels like too late of a starting point, and three years seems like not nearly enough time to make a difference. But God can do so much with what we feel like is too little. Even though Jesus accomplished a stunning number of things in His ministry, He didn't hustle. He didn't run around with His hair on fire. And He was never too busy for the purposes of God or to hear the voice of God. I mean, think about it: On any given day Jesus' schedule was packed. He had sermons to preach, places to travel to, people to heal, students to disciple, parties to attend, family obligations to take care of, and—not to mention—the inevitable cross of Calvary to prepare for. If I had all of that on my plate, I would surely burn myself out, drop the ball, and disappoint countless people. Heck, I've done all of that anyway.

How did Jesus manage to do it? He *was* perfect, but we tend to forget that Jesus was also fully human. He had physical limitations. He needed sleep. He needed food. He needed boundaries. He needed the strength of God to overcome temptations and struggles, just as you and I do. But the greatest thing He needed and prioritized was regular relationship with His heavenly Father. Even commissioned with the mightiest and most glorious of purposes, Jesus never lost sight of who He was or what He was living for. His Father God's mission set His pace, a holy pace, and eternity spurred Him on.

The reason Jesus was able to resist the urge to rush and hustle wasn't because His calendar was blank. It wasn't because He had no responsibilities and could just sit at home in total stillness. On the contrary! Jesus was sent by God to be the Savior of the world—to proclaim the gospel, to seek, to save, to rebuke, to love, to serve, to withstand ridicule, to die, and to rise again. Talk about a calendar that seems overbooked with glorious purpose! If there was anyone who had an excuse to feel overwhelmed by the demands of life, it was Jesus. Yet He never lost sight of who He was or what He was living for.

Look with me at three instances of how Jesus put God first before doing, in the middle of doing, and at the end of doing.

BEFORE

> "Rising very early in the morning, while it was still dark, he departed and went out to a desolate place, and there he prayed." (Mark 1:35)

We learn from this verse that Jesus thought ahead. With wisdom, He realized the day ahead would be busy. There would be people, tasks, and responsibilities to say yes to. But what He resolved in His heart to do first was to get up and get away.

The book of Mark describes the place He got away to as isolated, still, and away from distraction. Before He spoke a word to His disciples, traveled on the road, ate a stitch of bread, or drank the Jewish equivalent to coffee, He stilled His heart in a quiet place and acknowledged that the strength of God was the only thing capable of carrying Him through.

DURING

"Now it happened that as he was praying alone, the disciples were with him." (Luke 9:18)

It's laughable how often I think I can't be with God when I'm in a crowded room or engaged in an important task. I falsely believe that I can't be with God unless I'm holed up in my office alone, with my Bible splayed open, my pastel highlighters all in a row, and my son sleeping soundly. Although that situation is pretty sweet, Jesus showed us that we can still put Him first in the moments when we are with people or preoccupied by other tasks.

There wasn't one single moment when Jesus didn't need God's help, and there was not one single place where He couldn't send up even a short prayer. Our cubicles aren't exempt from fellowship with God. Our kitchen sinks aren't exempt from fellowship with God. Our cars in the carpool line aren't exempt from fellowship with God. Our desks where we vigorously type out a school paper, the gyms where we run and lift, and the chairs where we rock our babies to sleep—all of these are places where we can invite Him in and seek His guidance, even as we move through a busy day.

AFTER

> "After he had dismissed the crowds, he went up on the mountain by himself to pray." (Matthew 14:23)

Matthew's Gospel shows us what Jesus did after spending much time doing. Notice how he did not say that Jesus' busyness and responsibilities throughout the day were wrong. What Jesus was busy with was good. But Jesus knew that what His soul really needed after all that doing was refreshment. And that soul refreshment could not be found in food, in relationships, in sleep, or in experiences—however good all those things are. What He really needed was to seek the Lord after what I can imagine was a tiring and overstimulating experience. He needed to recover from the day by resetting His mind and heart, just as we do.

See? Putting God first is simple. Now, simple doesn't mean easy. What I'm trying to say is that the Word of God makes it plain for us to see. I don't know about you, but I can sometimes make things a lot harder than they need to be. The temptation is to try to squeeze Christianity into a rigid formula, but Jesus shows us that we don't need to do that to slow down and put Him first.

The solution is actually right in front of our noses. Only one thing is necessary. Only one thing will fill us and allow us to overflow into all the other categories of life: regular, rhythmic time spent with God, which happens by continually training ourselves to run in step with Jesus.

Don't Miss The Beauty

Michael, Hunter, and I call Oregon our home, and it is one of the most beautiful places in the world. (I feel like I can say that after seeing some pretty incredible sights across the globe.) Oregon is known as the Pacific Wonderland, an oasis of the most beautiful destinations. Cascading waterfalls; snowy, glistening mountains; cozy beaches; and rolling dunes. I have skied on the most glorious mountains, cliff-jumped into the clearest waters, hiked to the top of a roaring waterfall, and dug my toes into the sparkling sand. But more often than I'd like to admit, my obsession with busyness has robbed me of slowing down enough to truly embrace how beautiful it all is. Maybe because slowing down does not give the kind of results we tend to value—or so we think.

You can't rush a perfect sunset or a blooming flower. The dancing of warm colors across the sky, the budding and growing of ombre petals—this all happens as part of a bigger rhythm and process. The beauty happens in the middle. Life is made up of a thousand middles—middles that we often miss because we believe they are inconsequential, normal, or mundane. Yet God is just as present—and His purpose is just as exciting—in those middles as He is in the beginning and the final products.

God wants us to actively engage with Him in the process of things, in the rhythm of growth and investment, those middle parts that lead to the results we're yearning to see. When we actively resolve to put growing with Jesus first, the lesser things—which, yes, still need to get done—will be blessed.

This isn't like hitting the Pause button on your TV remote. Think of it as a regular rhythm or an open phone call. This is something that my dad taught me. He told me that he thinks of prayer like a phone call with God that starts the moment our eyes open in the morning and does not hang up until our heads hit the pillow that night. We may not be constantly dialoguing, but we can continue to come back to that conversation as the day progresses. The most wonderful news is that, even on the most jam-packed and overwhelming days or when we have the most hectic schedule in the world, if we will just continue to run back to Jesus, we can always count on Him to steady us. This happens in our whispered prayers. It happens in our minutes, moments, or hours in the Word daily. It's in our schooling, in our jobs, and in our homes where we aim to display the fruit of the Spirit. This is rhythm, a repeated pattern of open communication and relationship with God while we change diapers, pay the bills, make our dinner, talk to our students, hit a deadline for our company, or deal with physical pain.

Rhythm is not new or trendy. It was God's original idea, woven into the fabric of the world since creation in Genesis 1. God created the world in seven days with regular rhythms, routines, and rest, and we would be wise to live that way too.

The Big Three

Anyone who has planned a wedding knows how stressful picking vendors can be. Whether you have a big or small budget, it's challenging to decide who will help make your wedding dreams come true. When Michael and I were planning our wedding, we received some sage advice. We were encouraged to pick our "big three"—three nonnegotiable vendors or expenses that were most important to us. We decided ours were our venue, photographer, and caterer. This concept radically changed the way we planned. It gave us the freedom to let go of the other things that weren't our big three. It gave us peace in our budget, too, knowing that our money was spent on what mattered most.

Focusing our money on our venue, photographer, and caterer didn't mean that we didn't have a florist, decorations, or a dance playlist. It just meant that those things got less of our budget and our time and, in turn, our brain space that was already full of wedding plans and life in general.

Over the years, I've adapted this rule to shape my spiritual formation as well. My big three include Jesus (my faith, my Bible reading, my worship), my family (husband, children, our people), and my work. Again, this doesn't mean that other categories like community, friends, and church are not important. We regularly open our home during the week to host and often serve at church, and we couldn't survive without our friendships. But what this does mean is that, after taking a wise look at my life—coupled with lots of prayer—Jesus, my family, and my work are the three most important things I feel called to steward.

As I've gotten more disciplined about my big three, I've seen God's blessing on our family and on my work. When Jesus is my first love, my marriage grows. When I plead for Jesus to parent me first, I become a better parent. When I ask God to direct my work, aspirations, goals, and schedule, my tasks give Him all the more glory and I feel much less overwhelmed.

This is just one of the strategies you and I can employ as we gear up to get on the same speed as Jesus. Here are a few more to try.

STOP BEING STUBBORN ABOUT THE SABBATH.

A weary soul needs respite and rest. But not the kind of rest that happens every few months or years or whenever you finally burn yourself out enough to realize it. For those of us who long for a thriving relationship with God, we must prioritize rest to prioritize Him. We must weave rest into our lives as a sacred rhythm—key word being *rhythm*.

I used to see how long I could go without resting. I used to see the validity and beauty in Sabbath only when it felt convenient to me or my schedule. And I used to see rest as only one thing when, in reality, rest looks different for us all. The beauty of Sabbath, especially if it feels hard and grueling to try to incorporate, is that the more regular it becomes, the more doable it becomes. The more you enjoy it and look forward to it, the less burdensome it becomes.

Sabbath rest is one of the many ways that you and I can display our trust in God to care for us, our dependence on Him to draw us near, and our faith in Him to get done what we cannot. As Justin Whitmel Earley put it in his book *Habits of the Household*, "Sabbath is a whimsical rebellion against the idea that work is the only important thing in the world."[4] God is not limited by our to-do list.

LEARN TO BE OKAY WITH SILENCE.

I was able to get out of the house for the first time in a few days. I started up my car, flipped on a podcast, and pulled out of the driveway. Only two minutes into the episode, I frustratedly ripped my phone from the CarPlay cord and was met with silence. My brain was buzzing, reeling from the noise of my toddler's cries, the hum of the range above the stove, the taunts of my to-do list, and now this podcast. The noise was just too much. I drove into town with nothing but silence, and it felt amazing.

Silence is learned. It takes conscious effort and holy willpower, because we've grown so accustomed to the noise we live with on a daily basis. So we need to be intentional about countering that today. Ride in the car in silence. Turn your phone on Do Not Disturb. Find a time to sit with your Bible in silence. Eat dinner without the TV or radio on. These things feel simple and trivial, but they're practices that strengthen our spiritual muscles little by little.

Silence has the ability to bring our thoughts, questions, prayers, decisions, and worries away from a place of confusion and overwhelm and toward a place of greater clarity so that we can deal with them with the Lord. Silence reveals what's going on with our souls so we can replace the noise with truth.

ACKNOWLEDGE THE UNHEALTHY RHYTHMS IN YOUR LIFE.

Most of us would say we're generally honest people—honest with our spouses, our kids, or our employers. But when it comes to being honest with ourselves and where we need to grow, that's not always the case. That's something we need to change. If we want to pursue a Jesus-first life, we will have to accept the temporary discomfort of acknowledging unhealthy patterns, rhythms, and sin so that we can get to the healthy and holy growth that God has for us on the other side.

Ask yourself what overwhelms you about your schedule. Honestly evaluate where you are stretched too thin.

The Word should determine our schedules. **Our schedules** do not determine how much of ourselves we give to the Word.

Ask God to reveal to you how you are idolizing busyness and doing. Analyze your schedule and see whether spending time with God has been pushed aside to complete other tasks.

You're not alone. Every single day I go to battle with my paper planner. I still struggle with letting my planner determine how much time I'm able to give to God, when it really should be the other way around. The Word should determine our schedules. Our schedules do not determine how much of ourselves we give to the Word.

God, make us busy for the right things. Show us those right things.

BE MORE REALISTIC WITH YOUR DAILY TO-DO LIST.

Those words were hard for me to type. The problem with idolizing busyness is that we never feel like we can keep up. Life becomes a ride we can't stop. We become enslaved to our schedules and constant striving. But the truth of the gospel reminds us that Jesus put an end to striving. Everything that overwhelms us will start to lose power over us when we slow down and submit to God.

Practically, this looks like being both realistic and kind to ourselves when planning our days. Although there are way more than five tasks I must complete in a given day, I have challenged myself to write down only five things. For example:

1. Spend twenty minutes in God's Word.
2. Write a chapter of this book.
3. Respond to important emails.
4. Do Hunter's laundry.
5. Go on date night.

The most important things get on the list. Everything else is optional. If I get it done, great. If not, that's okay. Realistic isn't restrictive. Realistic is life-giving. Realistic means that I don't push God out of the picture but instead leave room for His grace and sufficiency to do powerful things through my inability.

DO SOMETHING TODAY THAT YOU WILL THANK YOURSELF FOR TOMORROW.

I started "closing down" my kitchen every night after seeing this trend on Instagram. The last thing we want to see in the morning is an overflowing sink and messy countertops. Am I right, ladies? It makes it harder for me to prep breakfast for Hunter, and the physical has a way of cluttering my mental space too. Closing down my kitchen has worked wonders for me, so I've been looking at the other menial tasks around the house or in my work that I could realistically do today that I would thank myself for tomorrow.

In the moment, doing dishes at nine o'clock when all I want to do is go to bed sucks. But the temporary suckiness of doing dishes for twenty minutes will save me from the overwhelm the next morning. This also allows me to not overload my schedule the next day and to do things that I can reasonably steward today. Obviously, there's grace in Jesus' name to leave your sink dirty or the laundry unfolded for another night. God will still be God if your sink doesn't shine. But making those small decisions today may just help you feel more present tomorrow.

CREATE MARGIN AND EXPECT INTERRUPTIONS.

One day just last week, I did not cross a single thing off my to-do list. Absolutely nothing. My childcare fell through, so my ability to check off my work tasks fell to the wayside. I beat myself up about it for a moment, until I looked back at the day. God did accomplish some pretty holy things during a day that I thought I had wasted. I refilled our homemade sourdough stash (served my family), read books (nurtured my mind), sang songs about Jesus with Hunter (discipled my son), spent prolonged time in the Word (filled my own soul), and went on a walk (moved my body for the glory of the Lord). All thanks to margin and God's redemptive plan for what I thought were interruptions.

Plan for space. Plan for nothing. Plan for open days. This gives you the space and energy not only to be expectant for surprising moves of God but to have moments of connection with God. Life improves as we give more space to what matters.

More Rhythm, Less Rush

He Sets the Pace

I'll leave you with this: The more you practice living rhythmically, and less rushed, the easier it becomes. The first time you refuse to conform to the world's breakneck pace will feel downright scary and uncomfortable. Do it anyway. But resist the temptation to change everything at once. Start replacing rush with rhythm at a pace that is sustainable. The more you do, the more life-giving results you will experience, and the more levelheaded you will feel in the midst of the chaos. Then the closer and more consistently you walk side by side with Jesus, the less overwhelming the mountain in front of you will seem.

There is refuge in the rhythm of Jesus. And whenever you fall out of step with that rhythm, know that all you have to do is look up to Jesus and look down into His Word to find His footsteps again.

He sets the pace. Our job is to run the race well.

Reflection Questions

1. Are you prone to letting busyness and hustle culture become distractions in your life? Think about whether you would consider your current pace more rhythmic or more rushed.
2. Oftentimes, we resist slowing down in life because we're afraid we are going to lose something or not achieve something. Be honest with yourself: What fear is holding you back from accepting Jesus' gift of rhythm and rest?
3. What is your current relationship with the principle of Sabbath? What kind of rest would be life-giving to you and help you to be less prone to burnout? Ask God to help you form a Sabbath rhythm, and enlist the help of trusted spiritual counsel to keep you accountable and give you suggestions on how to make this practical in your life.

TEN

Small Steps of Faithfulness

> *The greatest spiritual work happens in the normal moments of domestic life.*
> JUSTIN WHITMEL EARLEY

*H*i, I'm Tara, and I'm a recovering shover. (Say that ten times fast.)

Something you need to know about me is that I am a pretty organized person. Mess makes me miserable, and clutter makes me crazy. One of my favorite activities is to hole up in my office or bedroom and create a whole system of piles—a throwaway pile, a donate pile, and a reorganize-and-rehome pile. (To some of you, I sound like an insane person. But to others, I sound like your kinda people.) I get excited when we rotate out our son's toys once a month. I look forward to cleaning and packing up the old toys, choosing the next toys to rotate in, and then Tetris-ing it all back together in his tiny closet. It's like a fun game. My Instagram explore feed has started recommending cleaning products and organizational hacks for my home, if that tells you anything.

This leads me back to my confession of being a recovering shover. Let me explain. One late afternoon, I was meal prepping some delicious coconut curry for the week. I moseyed on over to a drawer in the kitchen, on a mission to find my can opener to bust open some coconut milk. It took an eternity to find that darn can opener. What I found instead were salad tongs, chip clips, scissors, sticky notes, phone-charging cords, old receipts, lipstick, and Hunter's crayons. I slammed that drawer shut in frustration and moved on to the next drawer. Lo and behold! There was the can opener—among ink pens, wrapped dog treats, pocketknives, and batteries.

Over the course of the next week, I started noticing that the can opener incident was not isolated. More and more things were vanishing, and I eventually found them in the most random places. *Why does this keep happening?!* Mentally, I began to connect the dots. I had developed this inexplicable urge, in moments of overwhelm, to shove things into whatever shelf or cabinet was close by. Dinner table full of stuff and friends coming for dinner? Shove it all in the kitchen drawers. Michael left his mail and ChapStick on the coffee table? Shove it in the hallway cabinet. Shoving was the fastest and most pain-free option—or so I thought.

The busier I was, the more overwhelmed I felt, and the more stressful life felt, the more I took to shoving. I wanted a clean house. I wanted a space that felt less overstimulating. I wanted to have some control over the chaos, I guess. The way to control, I believed, could only be through shoving and cramming. I was just too tired to put things where they belonged; so out of sight, out of mind. But while shoving gave me a sense of satisfaction, the feeling was all too temporary. I wasn't doing myself any favors in the long run, because I was just making more work for myself later when I had to spend an hour looking for an overdue bill that I had shoved into oblivion.

Why am I sharing this? Is it to encourage you to clean out your everything drawer? Maybe a little bit. Is it to remind you that your can opener belongs with your other kitchen utensils and not your phone-charging cords? Seems like a no-brainer. While those lessons are good, they're not the point. I'm sharing this silly story because it woke me up to a deeper reality.

When my life had reached a level of unparalleled overwhelm and when my relationship with God was at its most neglected, I had stopped doing the faithful, everyday work—the meaningful, behind-the-scenes work. It wasn't just can openers, bills, and ChapStick that were being shoved out of sight and out of mind. It was the little-by-little, day-by-day, obedient ways of showing up that following Jesus requires that were being shoved into drawers and neglected.

In a culture where going viral in a day and finding overnight success is on everyone's minds, the small, unseen, and gritty work is often overlooked. But that's just it: When you feel completely spent and absolutely undone, the last thing you want to do is more work. I get it. In the middle of my greatest seasons of overwhelm and distraction, the idea of adding one more thing on my to-do list made me want to cry. Honestly? I physically and emotionally did not have it in me to comprehend what kind of energy that would take.

Because of my tendency to rush and hurry, I wanted results, and I wanted them quickly. I wanted to be at the destination now instead of committing to the process. The truth is, in God's kingdom we do not come by spiritual transformation overnight. It is a daily process of moving forward that happens when we put forth our willingness, coupled with His mighty strength.

Just as in the story of the prodigal son, God does not expect you and me to be cleaned up instantly or go viral in our efforts overnight. In Luke 15:17–20 we read that once the Prodigal Son "came to himself"—or came to his senses—he went right away to his father, probably still very much smelling like pigs and looking like one too.

Friend, God is not unaware of, nor is He put off by, the fact that we are all works in progress. In fact, He delights in it. He delights in the growing, the shaping, and the sanctifying. He is a faithful, from-the-ground-up kind of God, and He is waiting to show you the miracles that arrive when you put in the faithful, everyday work.

Spiritual Math

The Christmas before Hunter's first birthday, my in-laws got him the cutest baby walker; you know, those toys that excite and entice babies to learn to walk. It was a helicopter with a powder-blue face and a propeller that spun, and it lit up with a bajillion lights and tunes every single time it was pushed. Hunter took no time at all to figure out how to push that walker around the house, jetting from wall to wall and dinging our furniture. But his excitement quickly overtook his physical abilities. His little legs couldn't keep up with his arms as they pushed. Michael and I tried to explain in ten-month-old speak that his legs had to keep pace with his arms, otherwise he would face-plant. And face-plant he

Small Steps of Faithfulness

did . . . many times. But with that experience Hunter learned a valuable lesson: Even though it's frustrating at the start, strength is built in the small, everyday baby steps. It's the consistent work that strengthens us for the bigger work, like running. And now I have a two-year-old toddler who doesn't stop running. See, buddy? That menial work really wasn't so small after all. Look at you go! It matters.

Taking consistent steps of faithfulness every day is a gift, but one that we usually don't consider a gift. How many of us, when we're overwhelmed and stressed out, try to take on even more? (Guilty.) I think back to when I was crying over my kitchen sink, thinking that cleaning a casserole dish at midnight was going to ease the stress of the thousand other things on my to-do list. But combating our overwhelmed souls and learning to keep up with God's pace instead of the world's isn't about adding more things to our to-do lists. It is often about subtracting what we have put before God and doubling down on faithfully showing up for what matters to Him. In doing so, the other things (that are still important, like doing dishes) are less world-shattering.

Consider the apostle Paul, one of the most influential Christian leaders, teachers, and preachers in history. When we think on his life, we often think of his big moments, like preaching to many and surviving that epic shipwreck. Yet we see that his days were filled with little and faithful tasks, too, like building tents for a living, sitting one-on-one with strangers, and spending long days traveling. In the flashy moments and the everyday moments, his heart was to be found faithful to God. He did not despise the little work. Rather, he leaned into it because he was fully convinced that God was weaving it all into a tapestry for His glory. Just like Paul, you and I can experience the joy that is life with Jesus—a sanctified string of little things that add up to produce the best work.

Our souls were created for a consistency with our consistent God that keeps us anchored to Him. Staying anchored, my friend, is how we keep up with God when we're just trying to keep up with life. We anchor ourselves not to external circumstances but to a God who is faithful to us and, in return, inspires us to be faithful to Him.

I will confess that I've relapsed back into what I call a "distracted dissonance" many times over the past few years, and each time I've come out of it, I've boldly declared that I am done putting Jesus on the back burner. But then what happened? My intentions didn't get me very far and I quickly went running back to putting the world before the Word. This happened because my foundation was shaky at best. I was not disciplined in my actions, and I was wishy-washy in my commitment.

So as you consider the importance of regular, small steps of faithfulness, think of it as spiritual construction work. When we invest regularly in consistent acts of faith, we're building a foundation—or reconstructing an established

Small Steps of Faithfulness

foundation—on the faithfulness of God. This foundation will help us stay the course when the enemy would rather us remain too overwhelmed and too overbooked to give God the time of day. Learning how to instill the right rhythms and habits creates a more trained version of ourselves and, as a result, leaves less of ourselves vulnerable for the enemy to attack.

Habits of the Faithful

Alarm clock blares. Eyes struggle to open. Hands reach for the phone. Fingers snooze the alarm and sleepily scroll Instagram. Eyes dry and glue to the screen. Distracted before our feet even hit the floor for the day.

Does this morning routine sound familiar to anyone else? Something I've been trying to make more of a habit in my life is not scrolling on social media or even touching my phone first thing in the morning. But to be perfectly candid with you, I have not been making much progress. It's not that I don't want to change; it's just that my desires have not been disciplined yet. Scrolling before I get out of bed every morning is fairly consistent for me. It's been this way for a long time, which is proof that habits are hard to break.

Think of a few habits you have during the day that are settled routines or regular tendencies (for example, drinking coffee in the morning, working out every day, watching an episode of your favorite show during dinner, listening to a podcast on your drive to work). What we habitually engage in during the day are life-forming practices. Habits shape us into a certain type of person. They are the different ways we spend our lives, and in turn, they reveal what matters most to us.

The beauty of implementing habits as Christians, when we use them to better our relationship with God, is that they free our focus. They free us from unworthy distractions and empower us to give our attention to what matters most, being fully aware of not only the present but the presence of God. They protect what matters most by putting boundaries on what doesn't.

But let's not get it twisted: Habits are not God. Habits are not the all-powerful solution to salvation and transformation, because only One holds that power. And I've learned the hard way that habits, however well-intentioned, can become legalistic if we are not careful or watchful. When our focus and emphasis shift more to the ritual or habit itself instead of how that habit will help us become more faithful to God (the ultimate goal), our souls suffer. Our relationships suffer. But habits, when approached as tools, can be helpful to us in the process of sanctification. It's spiritual formation lived out daily. Habits and grace working hand in hand.

Armed with the proper perspective of who God is and what habits are for, our commitment to God expressed through habits is a rudder that steers us into greater relationship with our heavenly Father. Habits are God-given tools that, if used wisely, can help us remain focused on Him when the craze of life would rather have us look elsewhere.

small steps of faithfulness

Not One-Size-Fits-All

One-size-fits-all clothing should be a crime. I remember shopping for back-to-school clothes with my mom at our favorite outdoor mall when I was in middle school. We wandered into a teen girls' store with the trendiest options. Bingo. I found the cutest jeans that I wanted to try on. I scanned the racks to look for my size, and instead I found the one-size-fits-all tag. It was on everything. The whole store sold only *one size*. Whose messed-up idea was that?

Life isn't one-size-fits-all either. The life that I have been given, with its seasons, circumstances, and routines, will not be the same as yours, hers, or theirs. I believe with my whole heart that the Bible calls every single person who has put their faith in Christ to obey the same commands, like bearing the fruit of the Spirit, for example. It's not only okay but beautiful if your season or the habitual practices that you put in place don't look like mine or his or hers. Rather, you and I can expect our seasons and practices not to look alike.

In 1 Samuel 17, as David was preparing to fight Goliath, Saul gave him his own armor to try on. We read in the story that "David put it on, strapped the sword over it, and took a step or two to see what it was like, for he had never worn such things before. 'I can't go in these,' he protested to Saul. 'I'm not used to them'" (v. 39 NLT). While our battle isn't literally fighting a giant in our backyard with some river rocks, David playing dress-up with Saul's armor teaches us something profound: What fits for some may not fit for others.

So the question for us to think about is this: What does your armor look like? Have an open and honest conversation with God about what your season of life looks like in this moment—what overwhelms you and your work, responsibilities, daily tasks, and the people you encounter—and what practices you can implement to best steward all you've been given.

As you're considering what habits might be most helpful for you to have more of Jesus right where you are, here are a few practical tips to think about.

CONSIDER THE TIME OF DAY.

Did you know that there is not one instruction in the Bible about the perfect time of day to do our Bible time? I wonder if God did not include that for fear of us turning it into something legalistic. To aid in forming daily habits of faithfulness, consider the time of day that you dedicate to reading your Bible. The psalmist sings of the benefit of meditating on God's Word at the beginning of the day as a way to start off on the right foot, and he also writes of how God was with him in the watches of the night, proving that His presence wasn't limited to the morning. Some of us may be more of a midday, lunch-break kind of person, or a relaxing-before-bed kind of person. When our habitual practice of spending time with Jesus is done prayerfully, consistently, and expectantly, we can expect it to overflow into the rest of our days and sustain us through the inevitable highs and lows ahead.

GET SPECIFIC.

The habits I have struggled to implement in my life are usually the ones that I was not specific enough in defining. Instead of having a general goal of "growing my faith," for example, it's better to get specific. Have a more detailed vision of the habit you want to implement, such as "I will read my Bible for thirty minutes a day" or "I will attend church and get plugged in to a weekly small group." It's a given that we all want to grow our faith, but how exactly are we going to do that in the details? Pause and take a moment to evaluate how you want to prove more faithful to God and the specific ways you can do that through your daily tasks.

STACK THOSE HABITS.

When I became a mom, my Bible-time routine drastically changed. I wondered how in the world I was supposed to wake up early, get a workout in, read my Bible, and so on before Hunter woke up. It seemed nearly impossible, until I learned the beauty and freedom of not only God's grace in changing seasons but the practical lesson of habit stacking.[1] It's a proven theory designed to help you build a new habit by identifying an action you'd like to pick up and adding it on top of a habit you already do.

For example, many of us have a cup of coffee every morning without fail (current habit), so try adding on a new desired habit (like reading your Bible more consistently) to your coffee time. Or maybe you wake up before the kids and crank out a workout. Add ten minutes of an audio Bible or prayer time on top of your workout or as you stretch and cool down after a workout. The goal here is to build upon something you already do, thus making your desired habit easier to implement.

START SMALL AND BUILD BIG.

One last encouragement on the subject: It's okay if you're starting small. I've said this before, but it's important to remind you of it again. It's okay if you're starting from zero. Things often start small, but what matters most about building daily habits of faithfulness is how you develop them over time. Just like increasing your weights when you squat or bench-press, you must start small because your muscles have not caught up yet. But the small begets the big. With every simple, daily yes of putting Jesus first, you're growing bigger spiritual muscles and strength. So take heart.

The Word of God is full of disciplined, faithful people, however imperfect they were. Daniel was a man of faith who got down on his knees every day and prayed, no matter what was on his agenda that day (including being thrown into a pit of lions). Jesus was able to withstand the enemy's temptations because He knew Scripture and routinely quoted it. The Proverbs 31 woman was disciplined and successful in her daily tasks because she was motivated by the glory of God and the good of her family. David knew God's Word because he consistently set it before himself.

Under God, and only under God, can routines develop into a wellspring of deep love and devotion. Routines cannot give life themselves, but they can invite the bettering of life when our hearts are willing to participate in the work of the Spirit.

Well Done, Good and Faithful Servant

In my prayer journal there is a section at the start of each new month to write down a characteristic of God that I need to lean on more or that I need to learn more about. Recently I flipped back a few years in my journal and found one month in particular that stood out. At the top of the page, it read "the consistency of God." Seeing those words teleported me back to the exact moment when I had first written them down. I was a tender Tara then, feeling out of control, completely overcome by life, and painfully inconsistent in her walk with Jesus.

The truth is, in the seasons of my life when I am the busiest, most stressed out, and most overbooked on my calendar, I have also been terribly inconsistent—in my workout routine, in my diet, in my mood, and most certainly in my spiritual disciplines. It's easy to see how I arrived at that point, right? When I don't give Jesus my time or affection each day, I begin to slip. With each passing day that I neglect my spiritual disciplines, it becomes easier to deem my Bible reading, prayer time, and corporate worship at church as less important.

As my fingers ran across the ragged prayer-journal page, the irony of it all hit me: Even at my most overwhelmed, I still knew, deep down in my soul, that I needed the truth of God's faithful and consistent character. After all, isn't that what we all crave? When we are exhausted from not being able to keep up, aren't we really searching for Someone who can? When we are overwhelmed by the mountain in front of us, aren't we really searching for Someone who is steadfast? When we are weary from unending responsibilities and calendar events, aren't we really searching for Someone who has no end?

Strung throughout the pages of Scripture are reminders of God's faithfulness, His consistency and steadfastness. We see it in His rescue of humanity after Adam and Eve sinned, in His salvation of the Israelites out of slavery, in His constant presence with them in the wilderness, and in His promise kept on the cross, just to name a few. God has proven over and over that He is not only true to His Word but wildly dependable and ever present for His people. Hebrews 13:8 tells us, "Jesus Christ is the same yesterday and today and forever." Jesus has never changed and will never change.

Isn't that the soul-satisfying truth that we need to cling to when life won't slow down, when everything is changing and our heads are spinning? God's loyalty, allegiance, and

When we are weary from *unending* responsibilities and calendar events, aren't we really searching for someone who *has no end?*

love are with you and for you. He is steady, unwavering, and unbothered. No matter how far we stray or how long we stay away, He is there to anchor us back to the reality that overwhelm does not have to define our life. An overwhelmed life is unburdened by the faithful character of God, who gives us the rest we need and a safe place to run to every day.

Let's make it our aim to reach the end of our days and hear the words "Well done, good and faithful servant" (Matthew 25:23). I once rather preferred to hear the words "Well done, good and successful servant," or "Well done, good and famous servant," but none of that matters more than faithfulness. None of that matters more than how I manage and steward the areas of my life well for the Lord.

When we switch from living overwhelmed to living consistently faithful, it changes everything. It reminds us that we have been deemed stewards—managers and agents of change—over the lives that God, the owner and our Master, has given us. That is wonderfully weighty work. When we grasp the reality that heaven is real and Jesus is the greatest treasure, it causes us to stop living distracted, weighed down, and hurried.

The Creator of the universe—the Creator of you and the One who sent His Son to take your place—is completely, utterly, and absolutely committed to you. He is the most faithful friend, Father, and helper. Just thinking about His everlasting, no-strings-attached love brings me to tears, and it brings me to my knees. And because He is all in for me, I want to be all in for Him. The faithfulness of God inspires

small steps of faithfulness

me to be faithful right back with my everyday habits and routines.

So the next time you're tempted to numb out and push Him out, the next time you're feeling so overwhelmed by your life that you break down in tears, remember that God is the surest thing you can count on. He is the heartbeat of your life that keeps you steady when everything else is shaking. And because of that foundation, you and I can find the strength to keep going and show up with the small acts of faith that actually add up to something big.

Reflection Questions

1. Is there anything that you have been shoving and neglecting as a result of how overbooked and overwhelmed you feel?
2. What are some of the seemingly small and mundane tasks that God has placed in front of you on any given day? How can you reshape how you see those tasks—from meaningless to meaningful—in the grand scheme of being faithful unto God?
3. What is one habit of faithfulness that you want to implement in your life?

Conclusion

I started this book with a story about me crying over the kitchen sink, so it's only fitting that I end this book with a story about me crying in a stadium of thirteen thousand women.

It was February. Dickies Arena, Fort Worth, Texas. IF:Gathering. 9:30 p.m. My mother-in-law and I sat with two of our friends in bleacher seats surrounded by women of all ages and walks of life. Jennie Allen, author and founder of IF:Gathering, had just set us all loose to turn to the person next to us and confess a fear or sin we were struggling with. Something we were concealing. Something we were too afraid to admit. But something that we might see freedom from if we did confess it.

You could feel the tension in the room as thousands of women squirmed in their seats, taking the brave and risky step toward vulnerability and healing with each other and God. I stared down at my shoes and admitted with a shake in my voice, "I feel like a fraud, and I'm afraid that God has called the wrong girl." When I admitted that terrifying

Conclusion

thought, I was questioning whether I was the right girl for the job, whether God was playing a cruel joke on me by telling me to write a book on overwhelm and distraction when I was still struggling with both of those things.

Not even a month later, I started reading a book by Ben Stuart and was taken aback by just how timely his words were to my uneasy spirit: "Your struggle may be one of your greatest assurances that you are alive."[1]

God did not call me to write this book for you because I had it all figured out. He did not ask me to be obedient and share this message because it was easy. On the contrary. I now realize that my struggle reminds me of the beauty that is my God-given humanity and also the beauty that is my constant need for Jesus and His ability to do powerful things through my weakness. Before I began writing this book and even while I was writing it, the Lord faithfully showed up in my overwhelm, living and breathing strength into my weakness. Does that mean I never struggle? Not at all. The struggle is proof that God is not done with me yet, nor is He done with you, because He is faithful to complete the good work He started (Philippians 1:6). That is the sweetest honey to my soul.

I get it. Putting Jesus first when you're already overwhelmed and overbooked is difficult, because we live in a world that is difficult. I firmly believe that you and I will never not experience bouts of overwhelm, exhaustion, distraction, and trying circumstances while we live on this imperfect earth. But in partnership with everything that we have learned together thus far, I want to leave you with this final thought:

Conclusion

Jesus is better.

Fun fact: Before we named this book *Overbooked and Overwhelmed*, I toyed with the idea of including "Jesus is better" in the title. Although I am 1,000 percent obsessed with the title we landed on, there's something profound about my original idea. "Jesus is better." That is the bedrock upon which this whole book stands.

> *The struggle is proof that God is not done with me yet.*

He is better than what is overwhelming us.
He is better than our overflowing calendars.
He is better than achievement and success.
He is better than social media.
He is better than comfort.
He is better than life.

The pace of life can be so crushing that it causes you and me to forget the supremacy and sovereignty of Jesus. When we find ourselves at our wit's end, it's often because we have forgotten that Jesus has no end. It's because our gaze has fallen away from Jesus and just how much stronger He is than what we are facing.

In Matthew 14 Jesus called Peter to walk out on the waves to Him, in the middle of a raging storm. With bold faith and eyes completely fixed on Jesus, Peter was able to do the miraculous. "But when he saw the wind, he was afraid, and beginning to sink he cried out, 'Lord, save me'" (v. 30). At first Peter was overwhelmed by his Savior's power, and that sustained him in the middle of the storm. But soon the

Conclusion

storm around him grew bigger than the presence of God in his mind, and that's when he began to drown.

Here's what I love about that story. I love Peter's moment of bold courage to even suggest such a crazy thing as walking on water. I love the commitment and constancy of Jesus to rescue Peter when he had a conflict of interest. And I love what you and I can practically learn from this story.

In the middle of the most overwhelming storms, what keeps us afloat are eyes fixed on Jesus, His power, and His presence. Because He is better.

What's incredible to me is that the storm never ceased for a moment. The wind and the waves were still beating the boat. Jesus had all the power to stop the storm and let Peter step out onto the water in perfectly calm seas, yet that's not what He did. He showed Peter that even during the most overwhelming of circumstances He was present, and His presence was His disciple's sustaining power.

Let this be an encouragement to you, my friend, that even though Jesus often does not remove the overwhelming situations from our lives, He gives us the gift of Himself to hold us steady in the midst of them.

What if we took heart, as Jesus shouted across the waves for Peter to do, when we're exhausted and overrun? What if we rested in the truth that Jesus is better and sweeter and more fulfilling when we are tempted to numb out and distract our souls with other things? What if we took a stand against a culture that tells us to overbook and overextend ourselves and, instead, exercised big, bold faith and walked at His pace?

Conclusion

Jesus reminded His disciples and us in John 16:33 that "in the world you will have tribulation. But take heart; I have overcome the world." Because of Jesus, you have not been overcome, because He has overcome the world for you. Because of Jesus, you will not be overwhelmed to the point of no return, because He has overwhelmed you with His love.

So as we fight for our relationship with God while trying to keep up with life, let's remind ourselves of the truths we've learned on this journey that can anchor us when we feel like we can't possibly keep up with life *and* Jesus.

- The solution isn't praying on your knees for more time and more things. The solution is cultivating a devoted heart and choosing not to let distraction win out.
- There is nothing wrong with enjoying the comforts, pleasures, and gifts of life. But we must be careful not to let those things take our eyes off Jesus, the Best Thing, or become more important to us than He is.
- One of the most loving things God does is not allow us to find true joy, peace, and satisfaction in anything less than Him.
- Knowing who God has purposed us to be is essential to flourishing and remaining firmly planted in a world that wants to steal our focus and tempt us to live for the temporary.
- Distraction is not a disordered schedule. It's a disordered heart in need of transformation.

Conclusion

- When you make Christ your home and when you put Him first in your life, you will see the weights, burdens, and overwhelms of life begin to lose their power over you.
- Limitations are license to give two of life's most precious commodities—time and energy—to the things of God.
- God desires for the wilderness seasons in our faith to shape us by elevating our awareness of Him and deepening our dependence on Him.
- The life we long for is found when we commit to not living so busy and frantic that we rush past Him and miss Him in our moments.
- An overwhelmed life is unburdened by the faithful character of God, who gives us the rest we need and a safe place to run to every day.

My prayer for you and for me is that we would not be overwhelmed by the road ahead but so overwhelmed by the love and presence of God, who walks with us on that road. I pray that we would feel a deep sense of freedom in our bones that enables us to walk with confidence, knowing that there's nothing and no one that we must keep up with except for Jesus Himself.

I love you and I'm with you in the fight to say yes to Jesus first—always and forever. But, more importantly, God is with you, and He is better.

Acknowledgments

To my heavenly Father—I am completely overwhelmed by Your love and presence, more so than I have ever been in my life. Thank You for redeeming every broken part of my story and transforming it for Your glory.

To Michael—I, now more than ever, can see why God joined us together. You have always held me steady, remaining confident in the goodness and provision of God, when I was sure life was going to take me out. For the ways you constantly affirm the Lord's work in my life and cover our family with security, I will forever be grateful. You are God's gift to me. I'm so overwhelmed (in a good way) that I get to call you mine.

To my boys—Hunter, my bright and brilliant boy. God has used you in many magnificent ways, teaching me how to truly treasure being present. Your childlike faith, dependence, and wonder inspire me. To baby boy #2, growing inside my belly right now, your kicks have encouraged me every step and page of this journey. You are proof that God

Acknowledgments

pours out unmerited gifts, and I'm overjoyed to step into this next level of motherhood because of the God we serve. You, my boys, are my greatest joy and proudest ministry.

To my family and friends—I hope you know how much I love you. Through every phone call, text, coffee date, conversation over dinner, gathering, prayer, playdate, or walk, you have filled my cup. You have seen me in my most overbooked and overwhelmed seasons, yet you have remained faithful. I honor you.

To my pastor—it's pretty wild how God fit a lot of the puzzle pieces of this book together because of your sermon on a Sunday morning. Thank you for preaching obediently from the Word and sending me links and notes from your sermons for research.

To Teresa, affectionately known as my "book mom"—thank you for being my wise and loving guide, helping me steward the messages on my heart from God and navigate the waters of publishing. You are truly a woman who knows God, loves God, and lives for God. I genuinely would not be here without you.

To Jessica Rogers—working with you has always been a dream of mine, and I am in awe that that dream came true. "Thank you" feels too little of a sentiment to express how grateful I am for your relentless commitment, creative vision, and loving refinement. Know that your work in strengthening this book will never go unnoticed. You are a wonder, my friend.

To the Thomas Nelson team—thank you for partnering

Acknowledgments

with me in birthing not one but now two of my book babies. Forever and always, working with you will be one of the greatest honors of my life.

To my online followers and friends—you are one of my "whys," given from God. This book is because of God and for you. I can't believe I get to do this. You inspire me.

Notes

ONE: DISCOVER THE DEVOTED LIFE

1. Shane Snow, "Science Shows: Humans Have Massive Capacity for Sustained Attention, and Storytelling Unlocks It," *Forbes*, January 16, 2023, https://www.forbes.com/sites/shanesnow/2023/01/16/science-shows-humans-have-massive-capacity-for-sustained-attention-and-storytelling-unlocks-it/.

2. John Mark Comer, *The Ruthless Elimination of Hurry: How to Stay Emotionally Healthy and Spiritually Alive in the Chaos of the Modern World* (Waterbrook, 2019), 55.

3. *Merriam-Webster Dictionary*, "breaking point," accessed October 24, 2024, https://www.merriam-webster.com/dictionary/breaking%20point.

4. *Oxford Pocket Dictionary of Current English*, "Full," Encyclopedia.com, accessed October 24, 2024, https://www.encyclopedia.com/humanities/dictionaries-thesauruses-pictures-and-press-releases/full-1.

5. "Full," Dictionary.com, accessed October 24, 2024, https://www.dictionary.com/browse/full.

Notes

TWO: THE COST OF DISTRACTION

1. Chad Ashby, "How to Stop Flirting With Sin," Desiring God, November 6, 2017, https://www.desiringgod.org/articles/how-to-stop-flirting-with-sin.
2. Jennie Allen, *Get Out Of Your Head: Stopping the Spiral of Toxic Thoughts* (Waterbrook, 2020), 10–11.

THREE: IDENTIFY YOUR CRAVINGS

1. Patrick A. Coleman, "Why Do Pregnant Women Crave Dirt?," *Fatherly*, updated January 31, 2023, https://www.fatherly.com/health/why-pregnant-women-crave-dirt.
2. "What Does the Bible Mean When It Says That We Will Receive a New Heart?," Got Questions, updated January 4, 2022, https://www.gotquestions.org/new-heart.html.
3. Dane Ortlund, *Gentle and Lowly: The Heart of Christ for Sinners and Sufferers* (Crossway, 2020), 61.

FOUR: REMEMBER WHO YOU ARE

1. "Social Comparison Theory," *Psychology Today*, accessed October 24, 2024, https://www.psychologytoday.com/us/basics/social-comparison-theory.
2. John Piper, *Don't Waste Your Life* (2003; repr., Crossway, 2023), 107–8.
3. "Come, Thou Fount of Every Blessing," Hymnary, accessed October 24, 2024, https://hymnary.org/text/come_thou_fount_of_every_blessing.

Notes

FIVE: CHOOSE THE BETTER PORTION

1. Marshall Segal, "You Have Time to Sit with God," Desiring God, September 2, 2021, https://www.desiringgod.org/articles/you-have-time-to-sit-with-god.
2. "Here's Scientific Proof Your Brain Was Designed to Be Distracted," *Wired*, August 22, 2018, https://www.wired.com/story/brain-distraction-procrastination-science/.

SIX: PRIORITIZE HIS PRESENCE

1. Sonia Fernandez, "New Study Reveals Changes in the Brain Throughout Pregnancy," University of California, September 19, 2024, https://www.universityofcalifornia.edu/news/new-study-reveals-changes-brain-throughout-pregnancy.
2. "Grey Matter," Cleveland Clinic, last reviewed on March 19, 2023, https://my.clevelandclinic.org/health/body/24831-grey-matter.
3. Brother Lawrence, *The Brother Lawrence Collection* (Wilder, 2008), 95.

EIGHT: A WORD FOR THE WEARY

1. Kelly Bilodeau, "Fibromyalgia: Exercise Helps—Here's How to Start," Harvard Health Publishing, October 13, 2020, https://www.health.harvard.edu/blog/fibromyalgia-exercise-helps-heres-how-to-start-2020101321153.
2. *Up*, directed by Pete Docter (Pixar Animation Studios, 2009).

Notes

NINE: MORE RHYTHM, LESS RUSH

1. "What Is Burnout?," Cleveland Clinic, February 1, 2022, https://health.clevelandclinic.org/signs-of-burnout.
2. Jess Connolly, *Tired of Being Tired: Receive God's Realistic Rest for Your Soul-Deep Exhaustion* (Baker, 2024), 51.
3. John Mark Comer, *The Ruthless Elimination of Hurry: How to Stay Emotionally Healthy and Spiritually Alive in the Chaos of the Modern World* (Waterbrook, 2019), 51.
4. Justin Whitmel Earley, *Habits of the Household: Practicing the Story of God in Everyday Family Rhythms* (Zondervan, 2021), 170.

TEN: SMALL STEPS OF FAITHFULNESS

1. S. J. Scott, *Habit Stacking: 127 Small Changes to Improve Your Health, Wealth, and Happiness* (Oldtown Publishing, 2017); James Clear, *Atomic Habits: An Easy & Proven Way to Build Good Habits & Break Bad Ones* (Avery, 2018).

CONCLUSION

1. Ben Stuart, *Rest and War: Rhythms of a Well-Fought Life* (Thomas Nelson, 2022), 32.

About the Author

Tara Sun is the uplifting host of the popular women's podcast *Truth Talks with Tara* and the author of *Surrender Your Story*. She is a dynamic speaker and creative, using her platforms to equip hundreds of thousands of women with the tools to know, love, and live God's Word in their daily lives. Tara's favorite titles are wife to her husband, Michael, and mom to their boys. You'll find them living and serving the Lord in Oregon.

Connect with Tara

TaraSunMinistries.com
Instagram: @MissTaraSun
Podcast: *Truth Talks with Tara*
YouTube: @TaraSun

Also Available in Audio

Listen to

Overbooked and Overwhelmed

in Tara's own voice!

An Imprint of Thomas Nelson

Available wherever audiobooks are sold.

More from Tara Sun

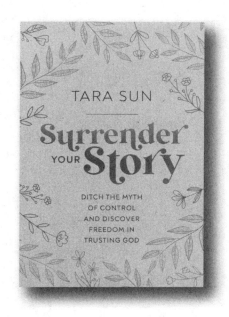

For those who are exhausted from trying to control their lives and disappointed by their unreached plans, *Surrender Your Story* is a welcome lifeline that will open your eyes to the beauty of a life surrendered to the Master Planner.

Available wherever books, eBooks, and audiobooks are sold.

The *Truth Talks with Tara* podcast is dedicated to helping you know, love, and live God's Word. Join Tara weekly as she encourages and empowers you to live out your faith by uncomplicating Scripture and providing Bible-based advice on life, relationships, and motherhood.